Spiritual Reading For The Average Christian

REVEREND ROBERT
E. ALBRIGHT

SPIRITUAL READING FOR THE AVERAGE CHRISTIAN

30 HOMILIES AND SERMONS

2008

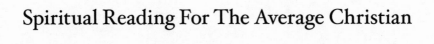

Spiritual Reading For The Average Christian

CONTENTS

INTRODUCTION / PREFACE

I am now retired, having served in the Roman Catholic Church as a brother of the Christian Schools for thirteen years and as a priest for the past thirty-five years. My ministries included teaching high school and serving as a houseparent in an orphanage while with the brothers, working as an associate pastor in two parish churches, and serving as campus minister at three different colleges and universities since my ordination as a priest.

The following sermons and homilies are a sampling of my thirty-five years of preaching in the pulpit. I have adjusted many of these works to serve as spiritual reading for you, the reader. You will notice these writings are categorized as sermons and homilies—the difference being this: A **sermon** is a talk or essay that explores a particular religious topic or issue; a **homily** is a talk or essay that attempts to interpret a particular passage or passages of sacred Scripture in contemporary terms, applying it to the lives of the hearers or readers.

As you go through the pages ahead, you can spot a **homily** by the required reading passage(s) at the beginning of the essay. It will be necessary for the reader to have a Bible handy to read the cited passage(s) *before* embarking into the homily itself. The **sermons** have no particular Scripture required, but contain Scripture passages within the essay itself. Biblical quotations in this volume (unless otherwise noted) are taken from The New American Bible, 1988 translation.

Throughout the homilies and sermons, various noted spiritual writers will be quoted. Who they are and the sources of their words will be explained in the text itself, without the need for footnotes or the like. I hope this makes for easier reading without the distraction of going to the bottom of the page or to the rear of the book, causing the reader to lose track of the thoughts, which are most important.

My hope in producing this little volume is not only to preserve some of the work I have done, but also to share it again with previous hearers and to expand to an even wider audience. In each of these pieces, I have attempted to challenge, inspire, and give meaning to the life of each of you, the readers. I pray that will happen! Thank you for opening yourself to me and all those whose words are contained herein.

Sincerely,
Father Bob Albright
January 2008

1.
OUR SPIRITUAL SELVES

Readings: Joel 2:12-18 Psalm 51 II Corinthians 5:20-6:2 Matthew 6:1-6, 16-18

The call of the Scripture above is a call to spirituality! The prophet, Joel, calls us to rend our hearts, not our garments (in others words, change our spirits, not our bodies). The psalmist who wrote Psalm 51 calls for a renewal of a steadfast spirit (in other words, to make our spirits willing, even when our bodies fail us). St. Paul, in his second letter to the Corinthians, calls them and all Christians to become the very holiness of God (in other words, wholeness = bringing the body and spirit into alignment with one another). Matthew, in his Gospel, tells of Jesus' call to the interior self and to avoid externals as a criteria for holiness (in other words, avoid hypocrisy = when your inner and outer selves are not in sync).

The call of Scripture is to a balance of our spirit and body—to wholeness—to harmony and unity—to holiness.

BALANCE—WHOLENESS—HARMONY—UNITY—HOLINESS are all one and the same virtue. **Spiritual activity** occurs when we Christians seek to wisely integrate the two sides of our person into one perfect human being. It is the activity whereby we evaluate our interior and exterior lives, our inner and outer natures, our spiritual and bodily selves. Spiritual activity is not to deny ourselves anything, but to give more to that part of ourselves we find more deprived than the other is. It is an activity to build up a faltering spirit or a weak body or both.

To accomplish this call to holiness and wholeness, one needs a **spirituality** (the new buzzword in secular and religious parlance today)—a way, a means, a discipline, perhaps even a system to accomplish what we have been called to as Christians. Every person has his or her own spirituality. Every religion practices certain spiritualities. Every culture has its own traditions or spiritualities. Spiritualities change from age to age, from people to people, from religion to religion, from group to group. Catholicism has many different spiritualities now and in its history. Alcoholics Anonymous has its own spirituality. Lutherans have their own, as do Baptists, Episcopalians, and all other Christian denominations. The American Indians, Hindus, Jews, Muslims, all have their own unique spirituality.

A spirituality is based on what answers you give to the essential questions of life: Who am I? What is my destiny? Where did this all come from? Depending on one's faith or philosophy or theology or religion or personal beliefs—a spirituality is formed in one's attempt to answer these questions. A spirituality is the way of life that corresponds to and carries out on a day-to-day basis one's faith or philosophy or theology or religion or personal beliefs. **Spiritual reading** is a way to sort out our spirituality or spiritualities. Spiritual reading is the time for me, myself, to go inward, to probe the depths of who I am—and also to go outward, to probe the limits of who we are.

In the pages ahead, we will explore the topic of **Spirituality.** We will learn its history, its diversity, its effects, and its future within the Christian tradition. We will examine other spiritualities such as Judaism, Islam, Oriental, Native American, New Age, male, female, and Creation. And so, these sermons and homilies are an attempt to help you, the spiritual reader, to enter into a time of introspection into your personal self and the life around you in the hopes that you will either begin a new relationship or strengthen your present relationship with God.

2.
CHRISTIAN SPIRITUALITY AS A JOURNEY OF SEARCHING

E very spirituality is an attempt to unite the human being with some greater force or greater being or divinity or mystery beyond itself.

Every spirituality is an attempt to help the human attain the fullness of humanity—to accomplish the greatest human potential.

Every spirituality is an attempt of humans to experience happiness and fulfillment in more than just the bodily, physical, and factual world.

Every spirituality is an attempt at wholeness, harmony, unity, intimacy, balance, and holiness between body and spirit.

Every spirituality has the same end in view, but the way and means differ from other spiritualities. In this sermon, let us talk about the same end. In the pages ahead, we'll turn our attention to the way and means.

For the Christian, then, spirituality is an attempt at intimacy with the God who has created us in God's own image and likeness.

One of the greatest spiritual writers of the last century, Thomas Merton, put it this way: "In order to find our own souls, we have to enter into our own solitude and learn to live with ourselves...because we cannot know (the human) until we find (the human) in ourselves. And where we find (what it means to be human) in this way, we find that (the human) is the image of God" (*Disputed Questions*).

To accomplish this end or goal, the Christian sets out on what we will call "The Spiritual Journey." The spiritual journey is a search for meaning that involves a search for both God and ourselves. Dom Hubert Van Zeller, OSB, in his book *The Inner Search,* says, "If the search after God is a drawn-out labour, the search after self is no less."

Searching after God and self is the quest of every Christian, which we call spirituality, and spirituality is no easy task. Matthew Fox, the contemporary Creation spiritualist, says, "All spirituality is about strength. True spirituality builds strength. It makes us strong for the spiritual journey..." or what Jacob Needleman calls the spiritual search. In his book *Lost Christianity,* Needleman writes: "To search means, first, I need Being, Truth; second, I do not know where to find it; third, an action takes place that is not based on fantasies of certainty—while at the same time a waiting takes place that is rooted not in wishful thinking, but in a deep sense of urgency. Without such a discipline, without such a search, even God is powerless to help people."

This seems as though a search or journey of this nature would be a lifetime endeavor, yet we have so many other things to accomplish in life, so many other things to do, so many other people to attend to, so many distractions. Van Zeller writes "To search after the face of (God) is a course which the world does not value. At best the world allows such a search a secondary place in a (person's) life. The world judges it proper that (people) should search after (God) sometimes (e.g., on Sundays or in times of crises)" (*The Inner Search*).

A real and true spirituality will not be impossible to fit into your lifestyle, but will become a way to enhance your life, make your time with others more meaningful, and help you accomplish all the other things you "have to do."

Thomas Merton says: "The vocation of the person is to construct his (or her) own solitude as an (indispensable condition) for a valid encounter with other persons, for intelligent co-operation and for communion in love. From this co-operation and communion—which is anything but the ludicrous pantomime called 'Togetherness' there grows the structure of living fruitful and genuinely human lives" (*Disputed Questions*).

And so, every spirituality puts us on a journey, a search. That search is ultimately for intimacy between God and us. But that intimacy cannot be attained outright. We must begin with an intimacy with ourselves that includes intimacy with other people and only then will we understand what the great Catholic spiritual writer, Tanquerey, meant when he wrote: "Spirituality is a science that is lived" (*The Spiritual Life*).

Let us also be clear about this search—what it is and what it is not: "The search is not for some new theology, nor for the return of ritual forms, nor for a considerate relationship to other traditions, nor for any broadening of doctrine to accommodate the changing problems of contemporary life. The search is for something 'smaller,' and at the same time more basic than any of these things" (*Lost Christianity*, Jacob Needleman).

By using the terms "small" and "basic" Jacob Needleman means the search is for a more important thing than theology or ecumenism or church doctrine. This more important or basic thing is the search for answers to the essential and eternal questions: Who am I? Who are we? What is our destiny? Is it to be separated from each other or is it to be a part of each other?

Only a spiritual journey, with some accompanying spirituality, will ever attempt to answer these basic questions with any truth.

If the end or goal of any spirituality is to answer the basic question, "Who am I?" then let's let the great spiritual writer of the twentieth century, the Catholic Trappist monk, Thomas Merton, have the last word: "The (human's) greatest dignity, the most essential and peculiar human power, the most intimate secret of humanity is the capacity to love. This power in the depths of the human soul stamps humanity in the image and likeness of God" (*Disputed Questions*).

NB, parentheses containing *italicized* words are titles of books. Parentheses within quotes are Father Bob's changes of the original quotes to make use of inclusive language.

3.
HISTORY AND DIVERSITY OF CHRISTIAN SPIRITUALITY

J esus had the most balanced of spiritualities! He could be found in the desert fasting for forty days and forty nights. He could be found alone in the mountains wrapped in prayer. He could be found at table with a few—on a hillside with a few more—or in the temple with a large crowd. We *hear* him praying on the cross, when performing miracles, while he is preaching, or alone with his disciples. We *see* him praying as he heals the sick, multiplies bread, blesses children, and carries his cross.

That Jesus gave his life, was martyred, crucified, and died for others became the source of the Church's earliest form of spirituality. The first Christians found it necessary to go to their deaths for the faith and so this became the way of living out the Gospel in a particular spirituality. Their spirituality was to die for their faith! As Christianity developed into a "world religion" and became synonymous with the Western empire, martyrdom was no longer a necessity and Christians had to look for a new spirituality. In the Gospel, they not only found the Jesus who *died* for others, but one who *lived* for others totally dedicated to no one but God. And so the Christian world began to develop a new spirituality of total dedication to God through celibacy. Monasticism flourished whereby men and women could go away from the world and live a celibate life of prayer, fasting and good works. Monks experimented, becoming hermits and living alone, outside the monasteries, not in communal life, but in total solitude. Sacrifice and self-denial in imitation of Jesus was the form of spirituality well into the Medieval Ages.

Those in monasteries (men and women) commonly practiced mysticism, fasting, intense prayer, and silence. As late as the seventeenth century this form of spirituality was still developing even into extreme forms such as those practiced by the Jansenists in France. The Jansenists were infamous for their contempt for the body in order to develop the soul's relationship with God. Mortifications such as scourging oneself, doing with little sleep and food, wearing hair shirts, kneeling excessively, engaging in sense programs, etc. became the normal spirituality for all those who wished to enter religious life. This prevailing spirituality up until Vatican II was one of denying the body in order to perfect the soul. And only a perfect soul could attain any union with God.

As we can see from our own history, much of the development of spirituality was done by nuns, monks, mystics, and those in organized religious orders—as they eventually came to be called. The spirituality of the ordinary Christian was ignored for the most part except to learn of monastic spirituality by reading or in church or in schools run by various religious orders. As became evident for us who lived through it—thrusting monastic spirituality on school children and the ordinary Christian adult in the world was not going to work. Vatican II, therefore, took on the task of a massive renewal of the Church at every level: cleric, religious and lay—theology, liturgy, and morality—pastoral, educational, and spiritual. A man on the cutting edge at that time wrote this poignant statement: "For the Christian, the purpose of life is union with Christ. This is no distant ideal proposed only to mystics and saints; it is an undertaking projected every time an infant is baptized" (*The Inner Search*, Dom Hubert Van Zeller, OSB).

Given our history of spirituality within Christianity and the Western world, our concept of union with God became elitist—belonging only to those who were religious or clerics. And even more, we projected spirituality as something only mystics and saints could achieve. So I think you can see that since Vatican II (1962-1965), we have just begun to explore, as a Christian community, the possibilities of having a spirituality or spiritualities for every baptized person. To do this, we have witnessed a return to our roots—to the Gospel—not history, not tradition, not the Church, not religion—but the Gospel, the Good News proclaimed, lived, and possessed by Jesus of Nazareth.

Christian spiritualities of the past have produced practices and exercises no longer palatable to contemporary society: e.g., the Divine Office, mental prayer, celibacy, clericalism, monasteries, convents, canon law, etc. Joseph Tissot, in his book *The Interior Life*, makes the claim, as do St. Ignatius and other great spiritualists in our history, that the fundamental principle of all Christian spirituality is Jesus Christ. Tissot says this: "Our artificial and superficial Christianity leaves Jesus Christ outside and on the surface. And He Himself declares that He wishes to dwell within the soul, and the soul to dwell within Himself. Jesus Christ is head and model of all Christians and He is the archetype of the spiritual life; what is fitting for Him is fitting, in due proportion, for all that springs from Him."

And so, where does our history of spirituality leave us? Where are we, as Christians, in our quest for wholeness, balance, harmony, unity, and holiness? Where do we, contemporary Christians, go to develop a spirituality that will be meaningful to us today? Do we leave the Church? Do we join another religion? Do we go on our own like the hermits of old? Do we repeat the past? I suggest the answer is no to all of the above questions!

I suggest we take seriously the words of Jesus: "Where two or three are gathered in my name, there I am in the midst of them" (Matthew 18:20). Then I suggest we take seriously our commitment as baptized Christians. Finally, I suggest we take our own intelligence, creativity, imagination, and experiences seriously. Put them all together and do this: Trust in yourself...Cooperate with God's grace...Form a community with two or three or twelve others who are also searching...Dialogue with one another on a regular basis...And begin to take the spiritual journey **together!**

4.
PRAYER

One of the essential ingredients (if not the most essential ingredient) to any spirituality is some form of PRAYER. Prayer goes hand in hand with our spirituality, which goes hand in hand with how we respond to life's essential questions, which ultimately goes hand in hand with our personality. Our personality is developed by givens and conditions in life. Our personality is what the Gospel calls us to develop. My personality is my identity, not my individuality. I am not interested in developing myself as an individual, but as a person.

Thomas Merton, in the book *Disputed Questions,* has this to say: "Individualism is nothing but the social atomism that has led to our present inertia, passivism, and spiritual decay. The individual, in fact, is nothing but a negation: He (or she) is 'not someone else.' He (or she) is not everybody, he (or she) is not the other individual."

Thomas Merton goes on to describe "the person" as the focus of spirituality—for a person is someone who wants to relate, to be for others, to live in community, to communicate, to pray. "The individual" is one who thinks and identifies oneself as separate, solo, unconnected, even isolated. Individuality is not the goal of any spirituality nor of the Gospel—personality, however, is. It is through my personality that I communicate. My personality even determines how I communicate or pray. Prayer is communication. We can pray to ourselves. We can pray to one another. We can pray to God. Prayer is personal. How I pray, when I pray, why I pray—all has to do with myself as a person.

Before I go any further in this sermon, I want to make something clear. I have no intention of telling you how to pray. How you pray will depend on you, as the person you are. Neither my way of prayer, nor even the ways of the great mystics may be your way. You must discover what that will be for you as you journey in your search for self, others, and God.

Countless spiritual reading books and books about prayer have been written in our tradition as well as others' traditions. Nowhere did I ever read an author who claimed his or her form of prayer anything but universal. Every spiritual writer gives you the impression that his or her method or way of prayer is "the way" to pray. Perhaps that's why so many of us never pray. We don't identify with those forms or ways of praying. Therefore, we don't pray. I know that was my own case. It has taken me over sixty years to develop a sense and form of prayer that has and gives meaning to me as a person.

Like you, I have been exposed to it all: The horizontal and vertical views of God affecting how we pray; the Gospel says "go to your room when you pray and pray privately"; the Church says go to Mass and pray in public; some pray every morning and evening, some before and after meals; some say the Divine Office, some do yoga or meditation or mental prayer; some pray always, others pray in need; some use formal prayer, others pray in their own words; some use contemplation, some engage in active prayer; some people pray, some just say prayers!

For John of the Cross, St. Bernard, and St. Thomas Aquinas, prayer was a ladder of ten levels toward divine love. For Adolph Tanquerey in the last century, prayer was a movement through the purgative, illuminative, and unitive ways whereby it progressed from prayers, to affective prayer, to infused contemplation. The contemporary Dutch poet and priest, Huub Oosterhuis, calls prayer by many names and ideas. He says: "Prayer is naive, waiting for someone who never comes...Prayer is monotonous, always the same words...Prayer is simply a matter of course in the Bible... Praying is speaking God's name, or rather, seeking God's name...Prayer is blessing, praising, giving honor to God...Prayer is remembering, recalling, anamnesis...Praying is a way of living, of waiting, keeping the door open, not having, asking" (*Your Word Is Near*).

For Huub Oosterhuis, the biblical authors and all the great spiritualists in the Christian tradition, prayer is synonymous with the rhythm of life. **To live is to pray and to pray is to live.** Then every breath I take becomes a prayer when I recognize that it is a participation in the life of God. Every person I encounter becomes a prayer when I recognize that it is communication with the presence of God. Every action I perform becomes a prayer when I recognize it as cooperation in worshiping God. Every pain I endure becomes a prayer when I recognize it as an integration into the suffering of God. Every success I achieve becomes a prayer when I recognize it as a celebration of God. Every prayer I make deepens my relationship with God. WHAT I do when I pray is the same as every other person who prays: I participate! I communicate! I cooperate! I integrate! I celebrate! I relate!

HOW I pray is where I might differ from other persons who pray: For I am white and not black. I am male and not female. I am Italian and not British. I am Christian and not Jewish. I am American and not European. I am a Westerner and not an Oriental. I am an extrovert and not an introvert. I am a believer and not an atheist. I am a Catholic and not a Protestant. I am a priest and not a farmer. I am a celibate and not someone's husband. I am...well...Tell me who you are—and that will tell me HOW you pray.

And so, my friends, what have I done in this sermon? I have tried to define PRAYER in my own words, as well as others in our tradition. I have not told you how to pray—for that is up to you. Prayer is so different for each person. What is left in this sermon is the most important ~ to tell you that prayer is essential and praying is something you should do. People are afraid to use that word should in our society. I agree that it is overused and has become a negative. However, if we use it to accompany a positive act such as praying, then I believe it is used well. Then let me repeat the most important message I can give you about prayer: You should pray! "Pray always" (Luke 21:36).

5.
A NEW SPIRITUALITY

All the great classical spiritualists in any and all of the world religions have given humankind a wealth of material for thought, prayer, reflection, and a possible spirituality. These classical writers and writings all come from a different world than the one in which we now live. Therefore, we, as contemporary Christians, must become careful and selective when we approach these classical writers and their thoughts.

WHY?

Because classical spirituality is inadequate for our world. Classical spirituality was based on life and knowledge in the past. That life and that knowledge were different and limited compared with how we live and what we know today. For example: The worldview in the Bible was a very simplistic cosmology. There were simply three levels of existence: heaven, earth and Sheol or the netherworld or under the earth. Life was simply body and soul, human and divine, good and evil. The earth was the center of the universe. People were the center of the earth. God was the center of creation. Religion, faith, myth, astrology, and all components that formed the Bible were contextualized in this simplistic worldview.

Today we know more than this. Today we have scientific proof that heaven and hell do not exist the way we thought. Today, we have knowledge about a much more complex worldview with a vast universe and maybe even more than our universe.

The questions have not changed—they are the same: Who am I? What is the goal of human existence? The faith has not changed—it is the same: For us, Christianity is Christianity (with whatever blend we possess by history and biology).

What is changing, however, is HOW to live the faith—HOW to answer the questions. That HOW we call spirituality! Within Christianity, we recall that the earliest spirituality was martyrdom, then celibacy, religious orders, living as hermits or in community, subduing the body to reach the inner soul. Today, our views of the body, life, and the universe are different from classical thinkers' views because we know other things they did not and we are different than they were. We need to discover a spirituality or spiritualities that speak *our* language, live *our* faith, correspond to *our* worldview, express *our* questions, hopes, and visions!

When we look at the great spiritual people of the past or read any of the classical writers, we should not be asking "What did they do back then?" but "What would they do **today**?!" What would St. Francis do today? What would Jesus say to *us*? What would St. Theresa write today?

WHAT?

When we compare or even contrast ourselves with our classical brothers and sisters, we begin to see WHAT the differences are. Classical spirituality was a journey from SELF to GOD with the exclusion of the world around us. Today's new spiritualities move from SELF—TO OTHERS—TO THE WORLD—TO THE UNIVERSE and then to GOD with the inclusion of all that is encountered in the spiritual journey. Classical spiritualities promoted SILENCE, were ORGANIZED into systems or steps, focused on the INDIVIDUAL, were GOD CENTERED, STATIC, FRAGMENTED, and sported an isolationist mentality to "go away," "go apart," "retreat," etc. Today's newer spiritualities promote DIALOGUE, are UNORGANIZED, focus on COMMUNITY, have NO CENTER or a CHANGING CENTER, are DIVERSE, HOLISTIC and tend toward INTEGRATION, to "go into," "be a part of," "belong," etc.

Classical spiritualities produced such great and worthy practices of piety such as the Rosary, Stations of the Cross, celibacy, fasting, penances, religious life, etc. The newer spiritualities have not yet given us any such practices. These are yet to be determined or will become too diverse to classify. Classical spirituality tended to change life to get closer to the mystery (e.g., by subduing the body). The new spirituality tends to get closer to life to get closer to the mystery and therefore teaches a balance of the body and the spirit. Classical spirituality operated in an isolationist mode: Doing it alone, separated from other cultures, religions, and people (e.g., Christmas excludes Jews and Muslims, or Passover excludes Christians and Muslims, or Ramadan excludes Jews and Christians). The new spirituality is more ecumenical, interfaith, and sharing: celebrating those things that unite us and not just the things that divide us (e.g., the seasons, light, birth, laughter, tears, love, relationships, relaxation, death, friendship, memory, nature, etc.).

THE FUTURE

The new spiritualities are not just repeating the past, but building on the past with a new future. The new spiritualities are not a break from the past, but an organic development bringing with them the fruits of the past, mixing them with contemporary creativity, and forming a spirituality that will span the twenty-first century.

Let us listen to some of the spiritualists of our own time, who are beginning to write the new spirituality. Listen to how Robert Wicks builds on the hermit and desert experiences of classical spirituality: "When we sit prayerfully in silence and solitude we are entering the desert, our desert. In this sacred space…(we) receive the grace to learn to face ourselves directly so we can learn to live ordinariness, to live ethically and generously with others" (*Touching The Holy*, 1992).

So living with others is a central piece of the new spirituality, and that means men living with women and women living with men. Listen to these words of the contemporary female author, Djohariah Toor: "Many of us have no roots as women; we lack an awareness of what feminine identity means. We have made long strides in the male corporate world, but these personal and social accomplishments have somehow only masked our confusion, and we still can't say who we are. Defined by roles and governed by agendas, we lose contact with the vital elements of our own nature. We lose touch with our feminine roots" (*The Road By The River*, 1987).

Robert Moor and Douglas Gillette address this same spiritual issue for men in today's society. They say: "(The world) needs to learn to love and be loved by the mature masculine. We need to learn to celebrate authentic masculine power and potency, not only for the sake of our personal well-being as men and for our relationships with others, but also because the crisis in mature masculinity feeds into the global crisis of survival we face as a species. Our dangerous and unstable world urgently needs mature men and mature women if our race is going to go on at all into the future" (*King Warrior Magician Lover*, 1990).

Bringing spirituality full circle, Dr. Danny Martin makes these observations: "Our present crisis is born of a distorted cosmology that attempted to separate humans from the natural order and present them as superior beings like the God they projected. In a new cosmology that is born of the scientific enterprise, no longer is the human separate; in fact, nothing is ultimately separate. In this conception, observer and observed merge and all become part of the web of one life process. In this world, humans are the universe now come to conscious awareness. The uniqueness of the human lies not in separation, but in being the carrier of the mystery" ("Soul Charter," 1994).

Finally in contradistinction to the classical spirituality based on "original sin," Matthew Fox has this to say: "We enter a broken and tom and sinful world—that is for sure. But we do not enter as blotches on existence, as sinful creatures, we burst into the world as 'original blessings'...Creation-centered mystics have always begun their theology with original blessing and not original sin...Whatever is said of original sin, it is far less hallowed and original than are love and desire, the Creator's for creation and our parents for one another. Our origin in the love of our parents and in their love-making, and the celebration of creation at our birth, are far, far more primeval and original in every sense of that word than is any doctrine of 'original sin'" (*Original Blessing*, 1983).

And so—what should we do now?—Now is the present! And these are exciting times. At present, we should strive to build on the past, but build a new future—always remembering that the future is awaiting us in our present attitudes and actions.

6.
BEING A DISCIPLE OF JESUS

For the Christian, Jesus is the most unique human being who ever lived! For the Christian, Jesus is the most central example of what it means to be human. For the Christian, Jesus is eternal life.

Why? Because, as John's Gospel states: "This is eternal life—to know the only true God and Jesus Christ whom (God) has sent" (John 17:3). And when we look at or come to know Jesus Christ, we find not only someone who had intimacy with God, but someone who taught and showed others how to be intimate with God also—"As you, Father are in me and I am in you, may they also be in us" (John 17:21). Jesus didn't reach intimacy with God for himself, but for others! "I came that (*you*) may have life, and have it abundantly" (John 10:10). The focus of Jesus' whole life and purpose was living for others—and because he received the strength to do this from the God with whom he was so intimate (so intimate that he called God, Abba, Father)—Jesus came to see and understand that *people, others*, was God's cause. The intimacy of Jesus with God was the source of Jesus' power and grace. His spirituality was so intense that the Gospel writer quotes him as saying: "The Father and I are one" (John 10:30).

The spirituality of Jesus was to find God everywhere—in the desert, on the mountain, in the temple, in the heavens, at the well, on the sea, in a leper, at a meal, on a hillside, with a crowd, in a Samaritan, sailing a boat, in a Gentile, breaking bread, among animals, picking corn, dancing at a wedding, on the Sabbath, in a synagogue, in a child, in a blind man, in a manger, on a cross, in a tax collector, in a prostitute, in Galilee, in the sick, in a Jew, in Jerusalem, in you and me.

To be a disciple of this man, Jesus, is to recognize God in the world and the world in God. To be a disciple of Jesus is to be at home in the world, to be at home in God. To be a disciple of Jesus is to understand that living for God *is* living for others.

But what does it mean to be a disciple? A disciple is a learner, a pupil, a student who engages in discipline that is instruction or education. A disciple is formed by discipline. A disciple learns by listening and imitating. Listening and imitating take discipline. Discipline is common to every spirituality. The spirituality of every Christian must be to become a disciple of Jesus Christ. Whatever spirituality we employ as Christians, it must always conform to becoming a disciple of Christ. Otherwise, we cannot even call ourselves "Christian"—for "Christian" by its definition means a follower or disciple of Jesus Christ. Therefore, the goal of every Christian's spirituality is to become a disciple of Jesus!

Now, what does it mean to be a disciple of Jesus? We need only to go to the Gospels to find the answer or answers to this question: Jesus, himself, said, "This is how all will know that you are my disciples, if you love one another" (John 13:35). "Whoever does not carry one's own cross and follow me, cannot by my disciple" (Luke 14:27). "None of you can become my disciple, if you do not give up all your possessions" (Luke 14:33). On other occasions, Jesus said this to his disciples: "Unless you become like little children, you shall not enter the kingdom of God" (Luke 18:17). "And pointing to his disciples, he said, 'Here are my mother and my brothers! For whoever does the will of my Father in heaven is my brother and sister and mother'" (Matthew 12:49-50).

Upon closer examination of these texts, we get a good picture of what a disciple of Jesus is: A disciple of Jesus is someone who does the will of God and not one's own will. A disciple of Jesus is someone who is as innocent and vulnerable as a child—yet strong enough to take up the cross. A disciple of Jesus has few possessions—yet possesses eternal life! A disciple of Jesus is recognized by others by the love he or she has for them.

But *what* does a disciple of Jesus do? A disciple of Jesus can be found making other disciples, teaching discipleship, modeling discipleship, celebrating discipleship always with a trust in the one we imitate, that when we live like him, he is with us and he lives in us. That is when we are true disciples: When Jesus lives with, in, and through us. "Go, therefore, and make disciples of all nations, baptizing them in the name of the Father and of the Son and of the Holy Spirit, and teaching them to obey everything I have commanded you. And remember, I am with you always, even to the end of time" (Matthew 28:19-20).

7.
DISCIPLESHIP

Readings: Leviticus 19:1-2, 17-18 I Corinthians 3:16-23 Matthew 5:38-48

A nd now let us examine the invitation or invitations we have all received as Christians to become disciples. We need go no further than the Scripture to hear that invitation or those invitations extended to us.

From the Book of Leviticus, the third Book of the Torah, God invites all of Israel to discipleship—"Be holy, for I, the Lord, your God, am holy." The Old Testament call to discipleship is a call to holiness, because God is holy. That's what it means to be a "disciple," to imitate, to live in the image and likeness of the one whose disciple we are. The Book of Genesis says we are all created in the image and likeness of God. The Book of Leviticus says that that image and likeness is "holiness." "Be holy, for I, the Lord, your God, am holy."

The Old Testament then calls all of us to "holiness" or "wholeness," which is a balance between the body and soul, harmony between the physical and spiritual worlds, unity among the diversity in life, intimacy between the human and divine.

The invitation to discipleship is a call to become "holy."

St. Paul tells the Corinthians that human beings are the holy temples in which God dwells on earth. He concludes that this holiness of ours will make us look foolish in the eyes of the world. Therefore, without using the term directly, Paul calls adherents of the Torah and followers of Christ "holy fools"!

The invitation to discipleship is a call to become a "holy fool"!

In the Gospel, "Jesus said to his *disciples*"—notice that what he said in the Gospel of Matthew was addressed to his disciples, and thus became his definition of discipleship. Jesus asks his disciples to do some pretty foolish things: Offer no resistance to injury—turn the other cheek—walk an extra mile—give more than is asked of you—love your enemies—do good to those who persecute you!

Again, as St. Paul reminded the Corinthians, the wisdom of the Gospel is foolishness to the worldly. Therefore, become a fool—a holy fool—and "be made perfect as your heavenly Father is perfect."

The invitation to discipleship is a call to become a "perfectly holy fool"!

8.

BEING HUMAN

Readings: Wisdom 2:12,17-20 James 3:16-4:3 Mark 9:30-37

Most of you have probably used, or at least heard someone use, one of these phrases: "I make mistakes—I'm only human." "I get angry once in a while—after all, it's only human." "She's only human." "He's only human." "We're only human." It's as if being human is something we would rather *not* be. It's as if being human is being inferior. It's as if being human is *not* what I am!

The use of the word HUMAN has been downgraded by such phrases and has lost all dignity. Yet, the Christian believes that God created people in God's image and likeness—if we are human, then *that* is the image and likeness of God. The proof of this conclusion is the coming of God into our existence. God comes as a human being, defenseless, innocent, the least among people, Jesus of Nazareth, a Jewish child.

It is Jesus himself who shows us what it means to be human. He reveals to us that the human and divine are not opposed to one another, but are intimately linked to one another. He, himself, is living proof, since he is both God and human. In Jesus, we have come to know and believe that God is human, and that to be human is the highest aspiration we people must have. To be as human as Jesus was, is the Christian ideal. To be a human being is the essence of Christianity. To be human and to be Christian are one and the same thing. To do as Jesus did, to be like Jesus is to be like God to one another. To be like God to one another is simply to be like Jesus, and Jesus was a human being. What is most like God is being human!

The Scripture readings above help us shed a little more light on this matter. In the Book of Wisdom are two classifications of people:

The "Just One" and "wicked." If we read it carefully, we would have heard the "Just One" described as gentle, patient, truthful, reproaching transgressors, and charging violators. Ultimately, he is called: "Son of God." The "wicked" are described as condemning, torturing others, testing others, finding just people obnoxious. Could we call the "wicked" "Son of God"? Would we call the "wicked" "human"? Is it human to destroy, kill, envy, hate? Or is that being INHUMAN?

In the Letter of James, this author too distinguishes between HUMAN and INHUMAN. He called jealousy, strife, inconstancy, vile behavior, conflicts, disputes, war, murder, envy, and squandering—he calls all these INHUMAN. What he calls HUMAN is wisdom, innocence, peaceableness, docility, leniency, sympathy, kindness, impartiality, and sincerity.

Finally, in the gospel, Jesus himself gives us a lesson on what it means to be human. He tells his disciples, if they want to be like him, they must become servants, as children, open to all people, the least among people. This is what they must do to be his disciples, to be Christian, to be human. Arguments, arrogance, killing, and self-importance are all inhuman.

Obviously, the distinction between HUMAN and INHUMAN is not always so clear, nor can we label one thing HUMAN and another INHUMAN without motives, feelings, and the like. Yet, it does help us with the meaning of the word HUMAN. We'll not as easily use that word to explain away our faults and failures. For our faults and failures make us inhuman. We become human when we correct our failures and ask forgiveness for our faults. We become human when we help others with their inhuman condition and forgive others for their sometime inhumanity.

Maybe we could change those phrases we started with to say this: "I make mistakes—I'm only limited." "I get angry once and a while—I have my limit." "She's only limited." "He's only limited."

To be human is also to be limited. We hurt and feel and suffer and die. We will not live forever. We cannot withstand all pain and suffering. We cannot be expected to be infinite, infallible, or eternal. But we must be human—we must love in spite of hate, we must hope in spite of despair, we must believe in spite of doubt. We must become free and we can do this only by freeing each other. (Jealousy, envy, war, hatred, strife, destruction—these all imprison people rather than free.) And when we are free, we will be infinite, no pain will stop us, not even death will separate us from the love God has for us. For to be free is to be human, and to be human is the image and likeness of God!

9.
LIVING VS. EXISTING

Readings: Wisdom 7:7-11 Mark 10:17-30

The word LIVE is also a word (like "human") that is attached to many situations and circumstances incorrectly. Let me explain! At the outset of our lives, we are given existence. We come to birth and we simply exist. Everything is given to us. We give nothing. Everything is done for us. We do nothing. However, we are not expected to be this way for long. We are expected to grow out of existence in order to LIVE.

Have you ever heard many old and sick people refer to themselves as simply existing? Have you heard middle-aged people say that if they ever reached a point in their life when they were old and sick, unable to live without life support in some hospital somewhere, that this is not living and they would rather die?

Living and existing are two different things! In the Book of Wisdom, the author praises prudence and wisdom over gold and riches, scepter and throne, health and beauty. We might think this foolish, yet if we look closely at these words, we learn the meaning of life.

The standard in the Book of Wisdom is the standard of life itself. To LIVE is to possess the qualities of LIFE! The qualities of life are those things that we can give to others to help them LIVE. Wisdom and prudence are life-giving, are life-supporting. Money, power, and comeliness are things I possess and contribute only to my welfare, to my existence. They cannot be shared with everyone, because they are limited, limiting, and they eventually possess us rather than being possessed by us. There is nothing we possess that does not possess us! Wisdom and prudence have no limit, because to really possess wisdom and prudence, one is prudent and wise enough to know that they must be shared with others.

In the Gospel of Mark, Jesus confronts the rich young man. The man asks to LIVE—"What must I do to LIVE?" Following the Law, acquiring possessions—these apparently are not what it takes to LIVE. (The man must have known he was only existing and he wanted to live). The young man can find no meaning in the Law or his possessions—so Jesus shocks him. Jesus holds out not only the words of life, but the words of eternal life as he tells him: "Go and sell what you have and give it to the poor...after that, come and follow me."

To follow Jesus, to give up all you own, to die in order to live, to live for others, to give yourself totally to people, to be God for another, to have nothing but life itself, to live that life to the fullest, to leave home for the sake of the Gospel, to suffer persecution for what you believe, to take the risk of loving, to believe in something, in someone, to hope that you will live for ever...THIS IS LIFE!

The difference between existing and living is our ability to give. When we give, we live! If we only take, then we simply exist.

It is easy to understand how an infant is not yet LIVING or how an elderly sick person on life support is not LIVING either. But how about us—we who are in the prime of our lives—are we LIVING? Do we give of what we have and possess (or at least the leftovers), or should we give up what we possess? Are we content to be wise and loving, or do we need money, good looks, and power to really feel alive? Are we LIVING because we can party, enjoy a sexual encounter, puff on a joint, or escape reality by dwelling away from home? Are we LIVING when we lose sleep, avoid work and study, seek one-night stands, become zombies, make ourselves sick from drink and a drag to be with?

As far as we know, life comes only once! Why spend life merely existing, taking everything, and giving nothing? Why spend life "doing what comes naturally?" "Doing what comes naturally" is sheer existence. Like an artist, we must improve on nature and LIVE. LIVING is: Loving, giving, sharing, growing, learning, becoming, forgiving, improving, laughing, singing, dancing, taking a risk, studying, believing, hoping, trusting, being for others, wisdom, prudence, selling all that you have, and following Jesus.

To LIVE is to become HUMAN!
To LIVE is to become like Jesus!
To LIVE is to become **yourself**!

10.
WISDOM AND FOLLY

Readings: Wisdom 6:12-16 I Thessalonians 4:13-18 Matthew 25:1-13

The contrast between wisdom and folly (the wise and the foolish) is much older than Israel and can be found in the writings and oral teachings of ancient Egyptian and Babylonian civilizations.

The Old Testament makes considerable use of this contrast in the Ketuvim or Writings, or what we Christians call the Wisdom Literature of the Bible.

Listen to some of these sayings about wisdom and folly:

"Wisdom builds a house...she calls from the highest places in the town, 'You that are simple, turn in here!' To those without sense she says, 'Come eat of my bread and drink of the wine I have mixed. Lay aside immaturity and live, and walk in the way of insight'" (Proverbs 9: 1-6).

"Folly is loud...she is ignorant and knows nothing. She sits at the door of her house, on a seat at the high places of the town, calling to those who pass by, 'You who are simple, turn in here!' And to those without sense she says, 'Stolen water is sweet, and bread eaten in secret is pleasant.' But they do not know that...her guests are in the land of the dead" (Proverbs 9: 13-18).

And so, in the Old Testament, wisdom and folly are rival sisters. Listen: "The wise are cautious and turn away from evil, but the fool throws off restraint and is careless" (Proverbs 14:16).

"Better is a poor but wise youth than an old but foolish monarch who will no longer take advice" (Ecclesiastes 4:13).

"Wise warriors are mightier than strong ones" (Proverbs 24:5).

"The fool says in his/her heart, 'there is no God'" (Psalms 14:1; Psalms 53:2).

"In the heart of the intelligent wisdom abides" (Proverbs 14:33).

"It is better to hear the rebuke of the wise than to hear the song of fools" (Ecclesiastes 7:5).

The New Testament takes up this contrast from the Old Testament, and in particular, the Gospel of Matthew, the most Jewish of our four Gospels uses the contrast like this. Listen: "The foolish person builds a house on sand" (Matthew 7:26). "The wise person builds a house on rock" (Matthew 7:24).

And from the Gospel reading for this homily: The 5 *wise* bridesmaids were prepared and ready to go into the wedding banquet, and did, while the 5 *foolish* bridesmaids were unprepared and not ready, and were left out in the darkness.

WISDOM and FOLLY
WISE and FOOLISH

An example of wisdom and folly from our own lives as students could be: students not being sure whether the professor will include a particular chapter on an exam or not. Wise students will study everything to be sure. Foolish students will study only what is sure. You've heard the saying: "Hope for the best. Prepare for the worst." This is wisdom. The opposite is folly.

Wisdom is light, that ancient fire, being awake, insight, awareness, foresight, being prepared, walking in light. Folly is darkness, that ancient abyss, blindness, uncertain, groping in the dark, being asleep and unprepared.

Remember, wisdom is not good and folly, bad! Wisdom and folly are not moral qualities! Wisdom doesn't mean you are smarter. Folly doesn't mean you are stupid. In the example I just gave, the more intelligent could look foolish and the less intelligent wise depending on their choices.

In the New Testament and for the Christian Gentiles—Jesus becomes God's wisdom to our world. The wisest thing God did for us Gentiles was to send us Jesus who is wisdom personified—and the wisest thing Jesus' disciples can do is to imitate Jesus. When we imitate Jesus, we possess wisdom, for we possess Jesus and Jesus is wisdom.

St. Paul reverses these images when he asks Christians to become "fools for Christ's sake" (I Corinthians 4:10)—in other words—to be foolish enough to imitate someone whose life ended in crucifixion. Why? Because then our hopes will be that God will do to us what was done to Jesus— that we too will rise from death and live with God beyond the grave.

Was it foolish for God to send us such a wisdom model as Jesus? St. Paul again reminds us: "God's folly is wiser than people" (I Corinthians 1:25).

So let us be wise and place our faith in God, the God who knows us better than we know ourselves; who also knows that there are times when being foolish will teach us a lesson and when being wise will have been only an accident!

11.

FEAR

Readings: Proverbs 31:10-13,19-20,30-31 I Thessalonians 5:1-6 Matthew 25:14-30

In the Book of Proverbs, we hear that the woman who fears the Lord is to be praised. Yet from the parable of Jesus in the Gospel, we hear that the servant who feared his master was punished while those servants who did not fear were asked to share in the master's joy.

What is this conflict we are faced with? In the Old Testament literature, fear of the Lord is rewarded, and in the New Testament, fear is punished! How can we resolve this confusion? Is it too simple to say that in the Old Testament, their theology was to fear God and that made it good—but in the New Testament, we were taught that God loves us and we should not fear God?! Yes, that is too simple and also perhaps a little inaccurate. The people in the Old Testament certainly believed in a God who loved them and saved them and had compassion. We find proof of this all throughout the Hebrew Scripture. On the other hand, in the New Testament, we find fear of the Lord also a good thing, since, as we read in Paul's letter, it will keep us awake and sober, since we know not the hour or day of his coming!

Perhaps, then, the answer to this conflict does not lie in a contest or competition between the Old Testament and New Testament, but rather in the meaning of the word FEAR! There appear to be two different meanings for the word FEAR in both the Old and New Testaments.

The meaning of FEAR found in the Gospel of Matthew is the one with which we are most familiar. The kind of FEAR the servant had for his master led him to do the wrong thing and thus to be punished. This kind of FEAR is fruitless and unnecessary, yet at times it overcomes us:

We have a fear of heights or a fear of dying or a fear of going blind or a fear of cancer or we fear a person who is mean, deceitful, and without mercy. Fear in this sense is the result of pain and hurt of which you are afraid. It can be defined as the apprehension of some impending evil.

But there is also another kind of FEAR—the fear spoken of in Proverbs. This kind of fear deserves reward, praise, and happiness. This is FEAR OF THE LORD! In this other sense, the word FEAR means AWE, to revere or venerate with AWE! To fear God or anyone or anything in this sense is to recognize the mystery as mystery, and when you can do this, you experience that it is too much for you so that you FEAR it, you revere it with AWE. Fearing God is knowing and experiencing God to such an extent that you "cannot take it," you cannot "handle it," you fear it, the mystery of God becomes too much for you. In this sense, you also fear life, not because it can be a source of evil, but because of its depth of beauty and mystery. In this sense, you fear yourself, because you remain a mystery even to yourself. This kind of fear brings happiness, blessing, and is to be praised.

12.
IDENTITY

IDENTITY is always confusing, painful, shocking, changing, overwhelming, elusive, surprising, helpful, uncertain, compulsive, revealing, unmasking...

The search for identity is the search for meaning...The search for self is the search for God...The search for the Divine is the search for the Human...We say of God the qualities and characteristics we wish *we* were—and yet we are! We say of Satan the qualities and characteristics we wish we were *not*—and yet we are!

Speaking about God is an attempt on the part of people to say something about ourselves...Speaking about self does not rival speaking about God—it is the same!

The answer to the questions, WHO AM I? and WHO IS GOD? is the same—it is an answer that attempts to give meaning to my life by identifying reasons, relationships, events, mysteries...

Israel said God brought them out of Egypt...I thought Moses brought Israel out of Egypt...No, Moses was God's instrument...If God is all-powerful, why did God need Moses??? No, Moses was so weak, that's why he needed God!!! Etc., etc., etc. An attempt to give meaning by establishing identity! What's God's job—what's Moses' job? Etc., etc., etc.

Christians say Jesus is God...Jesus says: "God, why have you abandoned me?..." God says: "You are my beloved Son..." Jesus asks his disciples, "Who am I?" Etc., etc., etc. An attempt to give meaning by establishing identity! If God says, "You are my Son"—why doesn't Jesus know who he is?

You see!—To some, Jesus has meaning only because he knows who he is. To others, Jesus has meaning because he *didn't* know who he was. But, you see—it is **you** (in the end) who determines meaning.

The meaning of who Jesus is—is not some objective reality waiting for you to grasp it—no, it is reality only *when* you grasp it with whatever meaning *you* give it. That's why Jesus asks his disciples WHO DO *YOU* SAY THAT I AM? There is no meaning for them if *he* tells them who he thinks he is. There is only meaning for them, when *they* tell him who he is.

Identity gives meaning!

They called (identified) him (as) Messiah, Son of People, the Way, the Truth, and the Life—even if they put those words in his mouth, and because they put those words in his mouth!

What does it mean that Ronald Reagan or Bill Clinton or George Bush is president? It means *we* identify them as such! They are not president because *they* say so—it's because *we* say so. I am not the leader and spokesperson of a community because I say so—it's because the community says so. Another cannot take my place without the consent (identity) given by the community. Once you give me that identity, then I can begin to have meaning for you. Once we give Jesus identity, then he gives meaning to us. Once Israel gives God identity, then God gives meaning to Israel. Once we identify ourselves as a community, then that community becomes meaningful to each individual within it.

Others help us define who we are. That's how others give meaning to our lives. Allowing others to help define who I am is the way I give meaning to their lives and mine.

13.
OBEDIENCE

Readings: I Samuel 8:1-22 Psalm 139 Ephesians 4:1-16 Matthew 26:36-44

Three times praying the same words: "Not my will, but yours be done." Who *knows* the will of God? Who *can* know the will of God? The Pope? Your boss? Your pastor? Your parents? Me? You?

I would like to suggest to you that no one can know the will of another until that other reveals it. You cannot know my will before I do! I cannot know your will before you do! To know someone's will and to have someone's will revealed to you are two different things.

I am suggesting, therefore, that the will of God cannot be known by us, but only revealed to us! I further suggest that, therefore, no one can know beforehand or at the moment of decision whether he or she is doing the will of God. The will of God, then, is not something we know and therefore we do—no, it is something revealed only later, afterward, after the fact, in retrospect.

No one knew this better than Israel—as is cleverly portrayed in the story found in the Book of Samuel.

As you recall: The people, Israel, wanted a king. Samuel, a judge and prophet, refused their request, reminding them that only God is their king. They still insisted that they wanted to be equal to other nations and to do this they would need a king. Now you see the dilemma and why this story is so important to us who claim to do God's will. According to Israel's theology, God lived and spoke in his chosen people—Israel. God also spoke through his appointed prophets and judges. Israel is the voice of God. Samuel, the prophet, is also the voice of God. Yet, these two claim a different and even conflicting will. The people say it's God's will that we have a king. The prophet says it's God's will *not* to have a king. Which is the will of God?

Well, we know what happened—they got their king, in fact, many kings. And after 200 years of the monarchy, there was civil war and Israel was divided into two kingdoms (not unlike our own North and South conflict in the United States). Then, after another 200 years of a divided kingdom, Israel was conquered by the superpowers of their day: Assyria and Babylon. The temple was destroyed, the priests were slaughtered, the king was murdered, and most of Israel went off to exile in Babylon.

It was at this point in their history that the story in the Book of Samuel was written down. The events, themselves 400 years old, are now written down and interpreted. This is what we call revelation!

In retrospect, after the fact, as Israel wrote the story of Samuel, they could now see what even Samuel and the people of his day could not see—the will of God. After 400 years of history, Israel could now see that it was Samuel who spoke the will of God, and not the people. Getting a king was the worst thing that ever happened to Israel—it eventually led to a loss of independence and destruction of all their dreams as a nation. The Bible *reveals* the will of God in this instance, but only *after* the fact. Samuel (at the time) did not know whether he was speaking the will of God, because there was just as valid a voice in the people saying the opposite of what he spoke. Therefore, it is only through revelation, after the fact, evaluating the results, seeing the consequences, in retrospect that the will of God is made clear.

It is the same with Jesus in Gethsemane. It is only after the fact, after the resurrection that the church can clearly see that Jesus was doing the will of the Father. Jesus was not sure of God's will, for on the cross he says: "Why have you abandoned me?" It is later, after the resurrection, that a story like Gethsemane can be written. It is in retrospect that the will of God is revealed. It is only then that Matthew can put into the mouth of Jesus in the garden: "Not my will, but yours be done."

And this brings us full circle to the passage from Ephesians. The author of this letter pleads with us to be humble, meek, patient, obedient, and most importantly open to the diversity that God has willed. The author of this letter pleads with us to create unity out of this diversity. We are to bear with one another, build one another up in love, and profess the truth. In other words, both unity and diversity are the will of God. This is the revelation we receive from this letter. No two people think alike, no two flowers look alike, no two animals have the same disposition; there are no two identical snowflakes, leaves, or fingerprints on the face of the earth. This is not just a fact—but I believe (like the author of Ephesians) that it is the will of God. **Diversity is the will of God.** Each person has something different to say, thinks differently, likes and dislikes differently, approves and disapproves differently, sees or doesn't see differently, hears or doesn't hear differently, is different than every other human being who ever was, is, and will be on this earth. This is the way it is—this is God's will. To try to change that—to try to make everyone think the same, dress the same, be the same, is going against the will of God. Not even God does that…Recall the story of Samuel again: Even though God's will was clear in Samuel's voice, God, himself, did not try to change the diversity found in the voice of the people. God permitted Samuel to go against God's will rather than destroy the diversity God created in the people.

So, what does all this have to offer us?

Obedience is a greater mystery than whether one says yes to one's human superior. Obedience must be to the will of God, to those things that have been revealed. Obeying a superior on the spot is not necessarily obedience to the will of God. Sometimes saying no is more obedient to the will of God than saying yes.

How do you know when to say yes or no? You will never know! How do you know when you are making the right decisions? You will never really know! How do you know when you are doing God's will? You don't know for sure!

Obedience offers no security—just the opposite. It puts us on the level of faith. We cannot be obedient without faith. Did you ever notice that when we are unable to explain something, we say it's God's will. Whenever we want something our way, we say it's God's will. We have made God's will our "cop-out." True obedience calls us to make our own decisions without blaming them on God or our superior. True obedience helps us to become mature, responsible Christians who have the courage to make a decision, and when it seems to fail, to be able to admit that it was our decision and not God's will. True obedience calls for the deepest faith and trust in ourselves, in each other, in God.

And so we go on, without answers to our questions, without knowing if we are right or wrong, without any assurance, but always believing and trusting in the God who brought Israel out of exile, in the God who raised Jesus from the dead, and praying with the psalmist: "My God, you fathom my heart and you know me...and yet, I still know nothing at all about you." (Ps. 139, as translated in the book, *Fifty Psalms* by Huub Oosterhuis, 1969).

14.
HOSPITALITY

Readings: Genesis 18:1-10 Luke 10:38-42

Among ancient peoples, and particularly nomadic peoples, hospitality was a strong tradition. The passing stranger was much respected and could always count on food and lodging. In fact, this respect was a religious respect! The entry of an outsider into the daily routine of primitive people seemed like a visitation from the sacred world of the gods. The stranger could be someone associated with the gods. He was mysterious; his welcome might win favor with the gods. And one never knew, the gods themselves might visit!

In Israel, this tradition continued, but with a new faith in the one God, Yahweh. You may have noticed the confusion in the reading from Genesis when Abraham sees three strangers and addresses them "SIR", as if there were only one person. This was Israel's new twist to an old tradition—no matter how many persons visited you, it was always a sign of the presence of the one God, Yahweh. For the Jews, such a visit by a stranger was a living reminder that Israel was once an enslaved stranger in Egypt, and in a broader sense a reminder that we are all strangers passing through this world. For Israel, then, a stranger should be loved, because in the Law (the Book of Deuteronomy 10:18-19), God loves the stranger. So then, Abraham is the symbol of Israel as he welcomes the three strangers, is immediately hospitable, and recognizes the presence of God as STRANGER as OTHER as TOTALLY OTHER. Abraham's hospitality was destined to become standard in Israel. Hospitality came to be understood as reception of the other, and thus a way of encountering the God of faith.

So, you see, it is in this context that we must understand Luke's Gospel story. And yet, even these verses of the Gospel alone are insufficient to get St. Luke's point. It is necessary to look at other passages to see what he is saying. Let's do that:

1. Think back to the story of Jesus eating in Simon's house—Simon was a Pharisee—Simon did not greet or treat Jesus as a Jew should—instead a sinner woman washes his feet in perfumed oil and kisses him—she is the symbol of hospitality to a stranger in this story as Abraham was in the Old Testament—Jesus, here, as in all cases in the New Testament, is the guest, the STRANGER. He is never the host (Luke 7:36-8:3).

2. In the next episode we find Jesus asking his disciples, "Who do people say that I am?" Their answer amounts to saying, "They don't know; you are a stranger to them" (Luke 9:18-24).

3. In the following story, Jesus is on his way to Jerusalem and wants to pass through Samaria—the Samaritans refuse him hospitality—once again he is a STRANGER, but this time a rejected STRANGER, as he himself states: "The foxes have lairs, the birds of the sky have nests, but the Son of People has nowhere to lay his head" (Luke 9:51-62).

4. In contrast to this story is the one where Jesus visits the town of Naim and raises a dead boy to life. The response to this by the people is, "God has visited his people." Here Jesus is a STRANGER, but recognized as God visiting his people (Luke 7:11-17).

5. Then recall the story of Jesus sending his disciples two by two as strangers into towns and villages to preach the Gospel—this being a sign to them that they too must be strangers if they wish to imitate him (Luke 10:1-12,17-20).

6. Finally, Luke puts the icing on the cake with the parable of what we have come to call, the Good Samaritan. In this parable, the Samaritan is the STRANGER (not Abraham, not Jesus, not a Jew, but a Samaritan). Jesus calls the Samaritan a "neighbor"—the parable calls the Samaritan a STRANGER—remember, this takes place between Jericho and Jerusalem (the home of the Jews and strange land for Samaritans). In this parable, the STRANGER acts like God, like a neighbor, and Jesus is suggesting to the Jews that God visits his people even in Samaritans (Luke 10:25-37).

7. That brings us to the Gospel above, where once again, in the home of Martha and Mary, Jesus is the guest, the STRANGER, and not the host (Luke 10:38-42)!

8. And to complete Luke's thought on this whole tradition, we must look further when Jesus says: "Ask and you shall receive; seek and you shall find; knock and it shall be opened to you" (Luke 11:1-13).

Have you grasped the point Luke is making? God visits people in STRANGERS—Jesus was a STRANGER all his life—Jesus is the greatest sign to us Christians that God has visited us!

There are some questions that these Scriptures pose for us, and I leave you with them to ponder and pray upon:

How many STRANGERS have you turned away from your life?

Why do we Christians have such a fear of STRANGERS when Jesus himself was one?

Are you a STRANGER to anyone?

Have you ever allowed God to visit you?

Perhaps the God we think we know so well isn't God at all—because **God is a STRANGER!**

15.

ABUNDANCE

Readings: Isaiah 55:1-3 Romans 8:35-39 Matthew 14:13-21

One of the themes in these readings is the theme of "abundance." In the prophecy of Isaiah, God is a God of abundance inviting all to come and partake of life even if you have no money. Isaiah invites Israel to partake of God's abundant covenant.

In the Letter to the Romans, St. Paul invites not only Jew, but Gentile as well, to partake of God's abundant love that comes to us through Christ Jesus, our Lord.

In the Gospel of Matthew—Jesus becomes God's abundance living among us. Let's take a closer look at this Gospel story to gain some insight for our own lives.

Jesus is apparently distraught over the death of John the Baptist and goes off to be alone, by himself. He needed to be alone—but then the crowds followed him. Yet he responds to their needs by curing the sick among them. It was in *his* moment of need that he responded to *their* need—and the miracle happens—their sick are cured. The message is clear—it is often at the moment of our greatest need that we are able to respond to the needs of others—and when we do—miracles can happen—our response will exceed our expectations—abundance is the result. Out of despair comes a cure; out of nothing comes abundance—but only when *we* are willing to give of ourselves, to give even the little we are able to give.

The second part of this story tells of the miracle of the loaves and fishes. There are only five loaves of bread and a couple of fish…That's all Jesus had to offer—yet, when he gave away all that he had, five thousand plus ate their fill. This too, is a story of abundance, of having more than you need.

I would like to ask a question: Was it foolish of Jesus to try to feed that large crowd with those few loaves and fishes?

Yet, he did it. He took the risk. He gave of what little he had and produced such an abundance that there was still some left over. How many baskets? Twelve!

How many apostles did he have? Twelve! The message again is clear: Jesus becomes the bread—for he is willing to share—willing to be shared—giving of whatever he *has*, whatever he *is* to his fellow human beings. It is not until he gives what little he has that the miracle of abundance really happens.

The twelve baskets left over are an invitation to his twelve apostles to do the same. Accepting Jesus' invitation will result in eternal life.

We are Jesus' apostles and followers too. His invitation is extended to us through the Gospel of Matthew: When we too are willing to take the risk of giving what little we have, we become like bread—broken and shared, passed around, eaten up, given away...And as we are consumed, we multiply and bring joy to others. We will satisfy their hunger; we will nourish them so that they too are able to give to others...

This is abundance! This is a miracle! This is eternal life!

16.
PERSEVERANCE

Readings: Exodus 17:8-13 Psalm 121 II Timothy 3:14-4:2 Luke 18:1-8

If you wish to accomplish your goals in this life, you have to persevere!

If you want to achieve anything worthwhile in life, you must persevere!

Perseverance is the name of the game.

Perseverance is necessary for the game of life.

Paul reminds Timothy: "You must remain faithful to what you have learned and believed...I charge you to stay with this task whether convenient or inconvenient...never losing patience."

Jesus tells the parable of a widow who won her rights from the corrupt judge, because she was willing to persevere. She never gave up. Rather than be worn down by the judge, the widow wore him down. He gave up. She didn't. He didn't use his stamina to win. She knew what it took to play the game. She wins the battle.

And how about Moses and Joshua! As long as Moses kept his hands raised up, Israel had the better of the fight; but when he let his hands rest, when he let his guard down, when he gave in, Amalek had the better of the fight. Again, perseverance wins the battle. Anything less is defeat.

At times, living is like a game and at other times, it is like a battle. In either case, it takes a great deal of perseverance to make it through life.

Routine, stress, and drudgery seem to be a part of living that often defeats us in our goals and dreams. Work is piling up all around us— at home, at school, at our workplace. Our aspirations seem distant and unreachable. A wall of despair and depression begins to replace the once clear-sighted and attainable resolve. We get bogged down with details and obstacles and sometime giving up is the easy way out.

However, piercing through all this comes a voice that says: "Pray… Get help…Stick with it…Don't give up…because you know who your teachers were!"

In our Christian tradition and history, we have been blessed with example after example, story after story, model after model of people who never gave up; people who had the courage to go on; people, who even in the face of death, never lost faith; people like: Abraham with God—Israel with Babylon—Jacob with the Angel—Jesus with his apostles—Tamar with Judah—the woman with the hemorrhage with Jesus—Moses with Pharaoh—Paul with the Gentiles—David with Goliath—Joan of Arc with the Church—The prophets with Israel—Francis with the poor—Katherine of Sienna with the pope—John Henry Newman with the hierarchy—Dorothy Day with the hungry—Martin Luther King Jr. with civil rights—Mother Teresa with the dying…And each one of you reading this can cite examples in your own lives of whom we could add to this list.

God's Word (the Hebrew and Christian Scriptures)…
Our Heritage (the Church and the saints)…
Our Pride (as Christians)…
Embarrass us when we waver…inspire us to go on…and equip us for every good work.

If I raise my eyes up to *these* mountains, then someone *will* come to help me!

17.

BEATITUDES

Readings: Zephaniah 2:3; 3:12-13 Matthew 5:1-12

About 4,000 years ago, a Hebrew by the name of Abraham made a covenant with God—an eternal commitment—that if he and his descendants would obey and proclaim the one God, that that one God would protect them and give them shelter from their worldly enemies in a land all their own. Throughout the centuries that followed, this covenant was lived and developed until it was ratified and confirmed in the giving of the Law or Torah through Moses on Mt. Sinai. This covenant became a relationship between the one God (who was called YAHWEH) and the people God had chosen (who were called ISRAEL). The promises made between God and Israel in this covenant are no different than the ones made between a bride and groom in marriage; or a priest and the Church in holy orders: mutual trust, care, and love, pledged forever.

Many centuries followed when the covenant between Yahweh and his bride, Israel, was broken and reestablished again and again. At a very crucial moment in the history between God and Israel, the covenant became all but over. The temple was destroyed, the priests were murdered, the land was plundered, and the people were led into captivity in a foreign land. It was at this most significant and horrible juncture of history that Yahweh sent prophets among his people to reform and redirect their hearts back to the covenant, by announcing a new covenant—not one written on stone, but in the hearts of Israel, deep within their being, as we read in the Prophet Zephaniah.

And so it happened as the prophets had spoken—another descendant of Abraham, from a small town called Nazareth, went up on a mountain, like Moses, and delivered the New Covenant prophesied centuries before. This covenant was both the same and different. It was rooted in Abraham and Moses, but became, through history and God's plan, a covenant for Gentiles, for all people—not just Israel.

That man, of course, was Yeshua (we call him Jesus), and that covenant was the one we read in the Gospel of Matthew—a covenant not measured by what you *do*, but by who you *are*!

This covenant asks people to be poor in spirit, be gentle, cry if you must, laugh if you wish, search for what is right, be merciful, prefer good to evil, pray, show hospitality, live in peace, be my people, be yourself, be human—but in all things love each other, even your enemies! We call this covenant the eight Beatitudes. We should keep them at our bedside and read them each night to determine which ones describe us and which ones we need to work on.

The New Covenant and the Old Covenant are the same, with one difference: The New Covenant includes all people, you and me, not only Israel.

A Jew enters the covenant with God by birth—the promises made by God to Abraham. A Christian enters the covenant with God by baptism—also the promise made by God to Abraham.

Whether through the water of the womb or the water of baptism, everyone who is in the covenant with God has certain responsibilities and commitments. For the Jews, these are carefully spelled out in the Torah, the Talmud, and the Mishnah. For the Christians, these are carefully spelled out in the Gospels, the ecumenical councils and the teachings of the Church. Added to the already existing mitzvot, or good deeds, spelled out in the Old Testament, the Christian of the New Testament is called to a life of virtue—not only *doing* good works, but *being* good!

The Church exists to help every Christian attain this ideal. Through the sacraments and ministry of the Church, we experience God's care for us. Through the reading and preaching of the Scripture, we experience God's love for us. Through the Church's teaching on justice, morality, and freedom, we experience God's trust in us.

The Covenant: Mutual care, trust, and love pledged forever!

So, here we are, members of the covenant, members of the Church—blessed and happy that God has not only shown us, but given us the way, the truth and the life. Now let's go out and live it!

18.

BEING SALT AND LIGHT

Reading: Matthew 5:13-16

You are the salt of the earth. **You** are the light of the world. Not **Jesus**, but **you!**

Jesus applies both images to his disciples. In other gospels, these images are applied to him.

In Matthew's gospel, believers in Jesus can be salt and light themselves. Jesus calls his disciples to a reality that is expressed in the images of salt and light.

Salt is what *we are*—light is what *we do*. Salt is being for ourselves—light is being for others. Salt is internal and part of who I am—light is what I become when I reach out to others. Salt is studying to improve my intellect—light is teaching others what I have learned. Salt is prayer—light is putting prayer into action. Salt is being a better person myself—light is being a better person for others. Salt is the female, receptacle side of myself, where I act as a vessel, a recipient of life—light is the male, outgoing side of myself, where I dispense what I have and share my life with others. Jesus calls his disciples to *be both*. A balance of salt and light is Jesus' call to his disciples, to us, his church.

To be the salt of the earth then, I must build up my very being through discipline, prayer, study, exercise, and all the good things life has to offer. I must make myself a worthy vessel, open to all the possibilities of life. I should take and receive food and ideas, accept the diversity that life has to offer. As long as I continue to be salt, I will never lose flavor.

To be the light of the world then, I must gather all I have taken in and use it for the good of others. I must be a giver of the good that has been given me. I should learn to live for others as well as for myself. I should teach others how to be salt themselves. And as long as I continue to be light, others will live because of me.

And now, let's get practical (as far as being a Christian). Being salt is studying your faith, attending church and praying to God in private. Being salt is taking advantage of the many opportunities to improve your faith. Being light is sharing your faith with others, bringing a friend to church, spreading the good news. Being light is modeling your faith by the way you live at home, and study in the classroom, and work in the workplace. Being salt and light is being what Jesus calls each one of his followers to be—completely human! Totally and wholly human!

And now the question arises in our minds—what exactly were Jesus and his disciples doing that would lead to this connection between SALT and LIGHT? What connection is there between physical SALT and physical LIGHT? Some scholars suggest that these are not just images for Jesus and his disciples, but actual physical realities that give way to metaphor.

In Jesus' time, animal dung and hay were churned together and hardened into bricks for burning fires—both outside and inside dwellings. Once lit, these bricks burned slowly and needed a catalyst or spark to ignite them further. To do this, one would throw salt on the fire. This would cause a tremendous bright yellow flame that could be seen for miles. It was, we think, in the course of this type of setting that Jesus made clear his message, for when he threw good salt on the fire, the intensity of the flame grew; when he threw bad salt on the fire, there was no reaction.

And now picture all of this and hear the Gospel with new ears and see the Gospel with new eyes:
"You are the salt of the earth. But if salt loses its taste, with what can it be seasoned? It is no longer good for anything but to be thrown out and trampled underfoot. You are the light of the world. A city set on a mountain cannot be hidden. People don't light a lamp and then put it under a bushel basket; they set it on a lamp stand, where it gives light to everyone in the house. Just so, your light must shine before others, that they may see your good deeds and glorify your heavenly Father."

19.
CHOOSING GOD

Responding to God's call involves making the decision to choose God! To choose God is putting God first in our lives. But what exactly does that mean—to choose God?

The decision to choose God means:

To choose to remain open to the opportunities that life offers, rather than remain closed and limited to only what *you* want.

To choose God means:

To choose to get to know yourself better, rather than defining yourself with cultural and societal definitions.

To choose God means:

To choose to live a creative life rather than a stagnant existence.

To choose God means:

To choose another before yourself.

To choose God means:

To choose reality over fantasy and realism over optimism or pessimism.

To choose God means:

To choose a relationship not just based on what you can get out of it, but also on what you can bring to it.

To choose God means:

To choose a career or vocation based on the gifts and talents with which you were created, and not on how much money it will make you.

To choose God means:
To choose faithfulness over success...

To choose God means:
To choose to forgive over holding a grudge...
To choose diversity and differences over rigid uniformity...
To choose freedom over slavery...

To choose God means:
To choose to live as a person of faith, rather than a matter of fact.

To choose God means:
To choose the Gospel over the easier ways to live.
To choose the Church as a means of living the Gospel.

To choose God means:
That in the end or in the beginning—or somewhere along the way—we must recognize it was God who chose us!

Readings: Deuteronomy 7:6-11 John 15:11-17

Questions for reflection: Why have you decided to follow Jesus? Why do you remain a Christian?

20.

BEING A PROPHET

Readings: Isaiah 6:1-8 Luke 4:16-30

How many prophets are there in your life? How many of them have you killed lately?

Once, long ago, before I was ordained, I heard a preacher in the pulpit speak out against the Vietnam War. His sermon berated the horrible aspects of war and its destruction. Shortly afterward, coming out of church, there was much dissatisfaction by certain members of the congregation about the sermon. The one specific comment made by two people having a conversation comes to mind—"I don't see why he just doesn't give a sermon on the Gospel," said the one. "Yes," replied the other, "the Gospel always makes for a good sermon." I thought to myself: He *did* preach the Gospel and these people didn't recognize it as the Gospel.

And it struck me! It seems we do not want to hear about ourselves—our mistakes—our hypocrisy—our wars—our crime in the streets—our friends drinking and on dope—injustices within our Church—dishonesty—loneliness—our Sodoms and Gomorrahs—parental negligence. We prefer to hear about the mistakes of (Moses and) the Israelites—the hypocrisy of the Pharisees in the Gospel—the people who did not accept the prophets of the Old Testament or Jesus, or his apostles (Herod—Pilate—the people of Nazareth). We seem content to allow our preachers to criticize others' problems and mistakes. However, the preacher is the prophet! The prophet speaks to people in and about the present and future...NOT about the past.

In the Gospel of Luke, Jesus said: "No prophet is without honor, EXCEPT in his native place, among his own kindred, and in his own house." And a prophet *is* in his own place when he speaks to people about the HERE and NOW—bringing meaning into all that concerns them, all that is right and wrong in their lives. We're all alike in this regard and I include myself—we don't want to hear about *our* apathy, *our* lack of concern for others, or that *we* are the "ME" generation. We become defensive and shut ourselves off, especially when it comes from the pulpit in church...I do this—you do this—it's a natural reaction!

Unlike the people who rejected the prophets of the Old Testament or who rejected the apostles sent by Jesus (in Jesus' hometown of Nazareth), *we have* accepted Christ into our lives—we believe! But very much like those people, we do not accept what he has to say. The message he speaks is the life he led. The prophet calls us to this reality. The Church, in its prophetic role within the world, presents the teaching of Christ to us. The Church, in its concern for the people of today and the future, must be willing to unsettle people from their apathy and greed for power— their concern to "save their own necks." The Church, as prophet, speaks critically about the world, points to injustices that plague us all. The Church must also be willing to criticize itself, to acknowledge its own mistakes, for only then can it survive, and, like Christ, present itself to others as a prophet.

But, who is the Church? You and me! The Church is people. We are the Church. Through baptism we are all called to be preachers and prophets and through confirmation we have been given the grace to speak out. So preach the Gospel with your lives! Prophesy by what you do! Give hope to those around you by accepting and living your vocation as a Christian, a prophet, a human being. This will make you humble. For humility involves a risk. And to take a risk is to live and die like a prophet, like Isaiah, like Jesus, like God!

How many prophets are there in your life? How many of them have you killed lately?

21.
BEING PROPHETIC

Readings: Jeremiah 1:4-5, 17-19 Luke 4:21-30

To Jeremiah, God says: I appointed you a prophet to *the Nations*— not just to Israel—but *all* nations—Gentiles as well.

Jesus, in the Gospel of Luke, cites the work of Elijah the prophet with the Gentile widow of Zarephath and the work of the prophet Elisha with the leper Naaman the Syrian, a non-Jew.

God keeps telling Israel that the God of Israel is everyone's God, not just Israel's. Israel fails to "hear" this word, this prophecy, and attempts to fight against Jeremiah and kill Jesus for reminding them of it. Notice—it is not Jesus' claim to fulfilling the Scripture passage that bugs the congregation, but only when he cites the prophets' preference for the Gentiles over the Jews are they filled with indignation.

God's promise to Jeremiah is, "I am with you to deliver you" from objection on the part of Israel. God's action in delivering Jesus from the mob in Nazareth is a sign of fulfilling that promise by God to all the prophets of Israel.

The call of God to the prophets is always a call to do the impossible, to become the victim of hatred, to be rejected, and possibly to be killed!

The call of God to Israel asking them to be a light or a sign to the Gentiles is finally fulfilled in Jesus, whom the early Jewish Christians saw as the light to Gentiles and glory to Israel.

Christianity went where no roads went—despite God's call over and over to Israel. Christianity went where no roads go—to the Gentiles—to you and me. Christianity has, since its inception, been a religion that bucks the system, be it religion, culture or politics.

The Church is called by God to be a prophetic voice:
-Aligning itself with the poor rather than the nobility...
-Proclaiming that might is not right...
-Lobbying against capital punishment...
-Fighting for the rights of the unborn; for laborers; for the elderly...
-Protecting the right to private property...
-Protesting the arms build-up and war as a solution to conflict...
-Promoting gun control as one means to end violence...
-Working for the rights of animals and environmental wholeness...
-Preaching and modeling against the "me generation" and the rise of individualism...
-Recognizing the good in all religions...

But, as a Church, we still have to go where no roads seem to be going in our own Church: Justice, equality, and a voice for women— Permitting the right to dissent as a moral obligation—Creating a safe place for homosexuals in our world...

"Large is the world
And long is time
But small are the feet
That go where no roads go
Go everywhere!" (A text by Huub Oosterhuis based on Isaiah 52:7)

22.
PREPARE THE WAY

Reading: Isaiah 40:1-5, 9-11

The literature of the Hebrew Scripture is in most cases very poetic, and like all poetry, needs interpretation. The writings of the Prophets, like Isaiah, are no exception to the deep biblical thoughts that people have pondered for ages and probably will ponder forever!

We have to remember that Israel sometimes saw their exile as a punishment for their sins—actually, as a result of their sinfulness. Notice what the prophet says: "A voice cries, 'Prepare in the wilderness a way for the Lord.'" The wilderness—the desert—the wasteland—the world without a liberator—the world without a purpose—the world living day to day with no direction—the sinning human race. The world must prepare a way! The wilderness must be turned into beauty and we must prepare the way. The world has become a desert of war, hate, killing, sexual promiscuity, idols, lies, disrespect, and lack of love. A place of slavery and exile. How can *we* make a highway, a straight path through this rubble?

The prophet continues: "Every valley shall be filled, and every mountain and hill shall be leveled. The windings and rugged ways shall be made straight and the rough ways smooth." Rugged land—rough ways—the jagged edges and the rough edges of *our* lives—the many faults that turn us into rugged land, deserts, and high mountains of arrogance. *Our* faults must be made straight. We must begin with ourselves. Our arrogance and false pride must be lowered. Our lives must be made wholesome and humble with inner peace. We must strive within *ourselves* to prepare—to work on the rough edges of *our own* lives, and then we can become a messenger to people—a herald's voice!

When *we* are people of mercy and justice—when *we* repent of our prejudices and apathy—then we will not only prepare the way, but promote the Gospel. For in the Gospel we find a man, a person, a liberator, Jesus of Nazareth, who has shown us the folly of sin. Sins kill—they put people to death or into slavery and exile. In him, we see a God who leads people out of exile and not a God who punishes. In Jesus, we have a symbol of a liberating God of mercy and love. For his resurrection forgave our sins. In Christ we learn that God lives in the midst of people, within every man, woman, and child.

Therefore, I ask you, are we the kind of people who live our lives in such a way that people can see God in us? Can we cry out with the prophets: "Here is your God"? Are we able to see God in others?—Even in our enemies?

So prepare—prepare, my people—prepare the way—for **you** are the way!

23.
FORGIVENESS AND THE NUMBER SEVEN

Reading: Matthew 18:21-35

I suppose that by now all of you mathematicians have figured out that 70 times 7 equals 490. Jesus told Peter in the Gospel of Matthew that he must forgive his brother or sister 490 times! Does that mean that when people commit their 491st sin, they should no longer be forgiven?

Let's talk a little about the biblical use of the number seven...In the Bible, we find the number seven used quite a bit—and also combinations of this number, as noted in the Gospel of Matthew.

The number seven, to the biblical writers, held a very sacred place in their symbology. To begin with, all numbers are symbols—they contain the reality they symbolize! In primitive Hebrew stories and folklore, the number seven symbolized other realities than the numerical quantity of seven. For Hebrews in the Old and New Testament times (and even today) the number seven had more meaning than math. Biblical scholars have noted four specific meanings for the number seven in the Bible:

1. When seven is used numerically, it refers to an indefinite or infinite period of time or times. A good example is found in the story of Joshua when God tells Joshua to have seven priests carry rams' horns while marching around the city of Jericho for seven days, and on the seventh day to march around the city seven times (Joshua 6:2-5). In other words—as many priests, times, days as it takes till the "walls come a tumblin' down."

2. The second usage of the number seven in the Bible is when reference is made to any kind of creation. The most obvious example is the seven-day creation story in Genesis, chapter one, with the seventh day being made holy—thus seven is made a sacred number at the outset of creation.

3. The third usage of this number is when any story of new life or new creation is told, such as the Noah's ark story and the flood. The flood is a symbol of cleansing the old evil creation for a new one, and so God tells Noah to take seven pairs of clean animals and seven days from now the rains will come to make a new creation (Genesis 7).

4. The fourth usage of the number seven in the Bible is when there is a message of hope as there was in every example I mentioned above. Hope in the infinite power of God to create us. Hope in the Hebrews conquering Jericho. Hope in God's mercy as God creates a new life after the flood.

The usage of the number seven in the parable from Matthew's Gospel is no different than the usages I just described. In fact, all four usages are made in this one story. St. Matthew, the Gospel writer, is a good Jew who knows his Jewish symbols well and uses them to the best advantage in his Gospel.

What connection, therefore, is Matthew making between forgiveness and the number seven?

Everyone reading this knows the answer to this question—because every one of you at some point of your life has had the experience of being forgiven for some fault.

Every one of you knows the feeling of relief and freedom one experiences when one is forgiven for a mistake. Forgiveness brings with it new life, being born again as a little child, being created anew. Forgiveness brings with it hope—for without forgiveness we would only despair—**as long as there is forgiveness, there is hope.** Each time you were forgiven, you experienced one of the great mysteries of life—one person giving new life to another; one person giving hope to another; one person reaching beyond the human into infinity.

And so, the connection is obvious! What, however, is the message?

The message is God's call to something new, some change, a need to look at old things in a new way—new life itself!

Because people are alive, they grow; because we grow, we change; yesterday we were children (seven), today we are adolescents (fourteen), tomorrow we will be adults (twenty-one). These fundamental changes affect and are affected by so many other things in our lives—especially our faith, what we believe! As children, we believed in Santa Claus...As adolescents, we found out there is no Santa Claus...As adults, we become Santa Claus...This is what it means to be born again...This is how an adult becomes a child again.

As our relationship with ourselves and the world around us changes, so too does our faith and our theology, which are rooted in relationships and this world. Therefore, a new phase in expressing one's faith is always growing in you and the old is dying.

Every chance of growth is a chance to start all over again—to be forgiven for our past sins and mistakes and to move into the future, new life. We do this at age seven, age fourteen, age twenty-one, every Sabbath, every September—every time we do this, it is an experience of the sacred number seven. So live, grow, change, become new, be forgiven, be born again seventy times seventy times!

24.
LOVING OUR ENEMIES

Readings: I Samuel 26:1-25 Luke 6:27-38

Let me begin by setting the passage from First Samuel in some context. Saul was the first King of Israel. David was the second King of Israel. Saul was a wishy-washy person who fumbled the government and made a fool of Israel in the face of her enemies. So God instructs the prophet Samuel to anoint a new King while Saul is still King. Samuel anoints David, a sheepherder and the youngest son of Jesse from Bethlehem. Now Israel has two anointed Kings—Saul and David.

In the passage above, Saul is pursuing David in the desert of Ziph. David, favored by God, goes into Saul's camp while he is sleeping—and instead of killing Saul, which he could have, he steals his spear.

David is the model King for Israel—he does not strike his enemy, but loves him as God's Anointed One. David respects Saul for who he is in the eyes of God and not in his own eyes. In the eyes of God, Saul is an anointed King. In the eyes of David, Saul is the enemy.

David, then, stands as a model for the Gospel of Luke, which asks us to love our enemies. That is why David is the greatest King in Israel's history; he had the ability to discern who his enemy was and see as God sees.

The Gospel calls all Christians to love their enemies, do good to those who persecute them, and bless those who curse them.

This exhortation and teaching of Jesus kind of turns the world upside down, and runs countercultural to what we learn in our classrooms, hear on TV, or experience from our government. The world in which you and

I live laughs at this Gospel as outdated and unreal. Very few people in our society live according to this passage in the Gospel of Luke. In our society when you lend something, it's always with interest...when we give we expect something in return...when we buy we want our money's worth...when we sell we always hope to make a profit...when we don't get what we expect, we take people to court.

In his day, Jesus was able to clearly define the enemy. In his society, the enemy was clearly the Romans who were the occupying force in Palestine at the time. Jesus was asking his followers to love the Romans. What we must do is define for ourselves who the enemy really is. Like King David, we might notice our enemy has two identities, the one *we* provide (which is "enemy") and the one *God* provides.

If then, we are privileged to see as God sees, we will no longer see an "enemy," but another human being just like us, with all the limitations and needs, with all the faults and goodness, with all the positive and negative sides. When David looked at Saul, he saw himself! The Gospel says—when you really see the enemy, then you will see yourself—so do to others what you would have them do to you! And remember—the measure you measure with will be measured back to you!

25.

HUMILITY

Readings: Malachi 1:14-2:1-10 I Thessalonians 2:7-9, 13 Matthew 23:1-12

When you are dissatisfied with something someone has done or is doing—do you find yourself asking a question or waging a criticism?

In the Scripture above, the prophet Malachi wages a criticism against the priests of his day. He accuses them in very strong language of not living up to the covenant of priests they received as members of the Tribe of Levi. I think we can conclude from this passage that Malachi is pretty *critical* of the priests he knew.

If we turn to the Gospel, Matthew seems to be doing the same thing—waging *criticism* at the Pharisees and scribes. He accuses them of being hypocrites—that is, not living up to the message they preach with the actions of their lives.

Both scriptural passages seem to be the words of frustrated men. They seem to have no other recourse but to *criticize*. Apparently, dialogue is out of the question. There is no sense of communication going on in these passages. It is clearly one sided: Malachi against the priests and Matthew against the Pharisees and scribes. No communication; only directed information.

The message today comes to us from those unnoticed words of Jesus: "Whoever humble themselves shall be exalted and whoever exalt themselves will be humbled!"

In other words—priests and scribes and Pharisees, who are humble enough to listen to those around them, will be exalted because they care what others think. Leaders who exalt themselves to the level of never needing to listen or ask or learn will soon be humbled by the criticisms of their followers.

The message is that no matter what our status is in life (priest, pupil, professor, parent, pope, or peer), we must be people who communicate, who listen, who learn, who dialogue, who become totally aware of the others with whom we share life.

When there is real communication, and we become dissatisfied, asking questions is the route we can take to resolve our dissatisfaction. When there is only information and not real communication, and we become dissatisfied, our only recourse is to criticize, which often solves nothing.

The heart of the Gospel message is humility. It takes a great deal of humility to listen to others and really hear what they are saying. It takes real humility to question without accusing. It takes true humility to learn from someone else. It takes a humble person to communicate the truth of what you know and feel to another human being. Being honest with yourself and others is a humbling experience. Humility is admitting that you *don't* know it all—that you *are* limited—that you *don't* have all the answers.

Where there is no dialogue, no communication, no learning, no listening—there is what psychology today calls a dysfunctional situation. In a dysfunctional situation, there is no one to talk to, no one who is listening, no one who cares. Malachi and Matthew are clearly in a dysfunctional relationship, each in his own time. When prophets and evangelists spot these dysfunctional experiences, they can only criticize and warn and speak out, since no one is really listening anyway.

Dysfunction results when people exalt themselves over others, dispense information without regard to feelings, see themselves as better than others, and never allow others their right to be heard. Dysfunction can be solved when people are humble, able to listen to and communicate with others, to see others as their equal, and to be aware of their needs.

The Greek prefix, **dys,** on the word dysfunction means ill or bad or difficult, to function poorly. Do you find yourself in any dysfunctional situations? Are *you* the reason for a dysfunctional relationship in your life?

Then you must learn to function with the humility with which Paul worked among the Thessalonians—being well disposed toward them, sharing with them, not imposing on them in any way, being as gentle as any nursing mother fondling her little ones.

But if you find yourself in a situation that does not allow you to be humble like Paul, then join the ranks of Malachi and Matthew and wage the kind of criticism that comes not with words, but with good example.

26.

SALVATION IS FOR EVERYONE

Readings: Colossians 1:12-20 Luke 23:35-43

According to all Christian theology—from the most radical to the most conservative—from the first century to the present century—the death of Jesus brought salvation to this world of ours! St. Luke, in the story above, captured this theology in a colorful moment between Jesus and the so-called "good thief." In the mouth of Jesus, Luke places those immortal words: "I assure you, this day you will be with me in paradise." Not even a thief escapes the salvation Jesus brings.

In Paul's letter to the Colossians, this theology is even more poignant as he tells those Greeks: "It pleased God to make absolute fullness reside in Jesus the Christ, and, by means of him, to reconcile everything in his person, everything, I say, both on earth and in the heavens, making peace through the blood of his cross."

Now, how do you fight with all of that?! Yet, some Christians do! Some people would lead us to believe that these words have conditions attached to them. Even the official Church down through the centuries has created conditions for salvation. In our own day, rigid factions within Christianity have relegated to damnation all persons who disagree with them.

Are they saying the crucifixion didn't work? Are they saying God places conditions on salvation? Are they saying that people are more powerful than God? Are they saying that they speak on behalf of God? According to another universally accepted Christian theology—God speaks through the Bible! And unless my eyes and ears deceived me, I don't remember Jesus asking anything of the thief in return, nor placing any conditions on his entry into paradise. Rev. Billy Graham, in one of his sermons, once said "I expect to see that thief in heaven." In another letter of his, Paul states:

"While we were yet sinners, Christ died for us" (Romans 5:8). And in the letter to the Colossians—"God rescued us from the power of darkness, and brought us into the Kingdom of God's beloved Son, through whom we have redemption, the forgiveness of our sins."

My former theological mentor, Father Felix Malmberg, SJ, used to say—"Either Jesus saved us all or he didn't. If he saved us, and I believe with Paul he did, then I also believe with Paul that he saved **all** people." Paul says in Colossians: "...to reconcile everything in his person, **everything,** I say, both on earth and in the heavens..." And that doesn't just mean white people, or Gentiles, or heterosexuals, or church attendees, or Christians, or Catholics! NOT AT ALL—that means **everyone and everything**—we have been reconciled right down to the core of the universe.

For a moment, let's lay aside the psychological, historical, political, and cultural dimensions of the Christian Church for the past two thousand years, and analyze the Hebrew and Christian Scriptures. In the Book of Exodus, God's first great act of salvation takes place when Moses is able to lead the Hebrews out of slavery in Egypt to the Promised Land. Nowhere in this story are conditions placed on the Hebrews before this exodus can happen. Yet, it does happen! God freely chooses to save without demanding anything in return. Once the Hebrews recognized through faith this act of God on their behalf, then they responded by entering into a covenant with God and becoming Israel. The Exodus came first—the covenant came second! Salvation came first—response came afterward! God saves—people respond.

In the four Gospels of the Christian Testament, God's great act of salvation is in the life, death, and resurrection of Jesus. Nowhere in this story are conditions placed on people before it can happen. Yet it does happen! God freely chooses to save again without demanding anything in return. Once the Jews recognized in faith this act of God on their behalf, then they responded by forming the Church and becoming Christians! The Crucifixion came first—the Church came second! Salvation came first—response came afterward! God saves—people respond.

The institutions of Judaism and Christianity are responses to God's saving work in our world, not conditions for salvation. What then is an authentic response to salvation (And by authentic, I mean, found in Scripture and tradition)? The authentic response is to make that salvation known from age to age, from people to people—and not to claim salvation as your own! Religion must never set itself up as the dispenser of salvation or the prerequisite for salvation, but only as a vehicle for salvation in the here and now of people. Religion must make known what she believes God has already done, is doing, and will continue to do—to save us without any demands. Religion is the bearer of the message, the servant of people, and the shepherd that guards the faithful—not rulers, judges, and kings! Religion, in imitation of the salvation it has responded to, must liberate and free people and not alienate them.

And so, it is in this spirit that we who are members of the Christian religion must learn to be proud of our religion—not to apologize for it when some divert it from its authentic path, but to be examples ourselves of what we believe, and hope that this example can become a source of salvation for those who wish to receive it.

27.
OUR BODILY SELVES

On Ash Wednesday all over the world, many Christians emerge from their churches wearing ashes on their foreheads. Some people might think this a strange custom, but ashes symbolize the "bodiliness" or the physical in human nature. Ashes indicate (very pointedly) that people are bodies as well as spirits. To go even further, being physical bodies is already a symbol (by itself) of who, in reality, we are.

Part of that reality becomes clearer as we realize our attractiveness to the physical: A sunset, moon glow, pizza, the naked human body, chocolate, or Mozart. We **are** physical—we **appreciate** the physical—we sometimes even **desire** the physical! In our awareness of the physical around us and how separate our own bodies are from it, we yearn to do more than just reach out or touch or see or hear or taste or feel…It is here that we discover our sexuality, because we seek intercourse with nature and people; we desire oneness with life and love; we look for intimacy with one another; we form relationships, friendships, and marriages. We act out our sexuality! Yes, we are sexual beings and all that this implies. But sexuality is more than the genitals. Sexuality reaches deep into the core of every human being—it is like a fire in the center of the earth or the sun at the center of the solar system. It is the curiosity behind every search, the inertia behind every desire, the force behind every action. At the risk of sounding somewhat Freudian, we could say that sexuality is the *outward* expression of the total self—everything you are.

The sexual act is an act of mutual response between two people who experience this act as a good. Therefore, the more intimate we get sexually, the more committed we need be to each other—and thus we form a covenant. Maybe more than in any other physical act, the sexual act is where we tangibly experience the full meaning of a covenant. That full meaning being the interplay between freedom and commitment.

REVEREND ROBERT E. ALBRIGHT

Commitment and freedom are elusive concepts. We want to be free, yet we do not know how. Often in the process of seeking freedom, we dispense with any kind of commitment or response-ability. Israel learned early on that God saves, but they must do something too. They cannot just receive without giving in return. Thus, the covenant was formed. We are free only if we are committed! The sexual act can make us free only if we are committed to the other person—otherwise we experience only temporary satisfaction.

Like Israel, we Christians too are people of the covenant. We have committed ourselves to model our lives on Israel's relationship with God. We are not just any people who are capable of the sexual act; we are a baptized people operating out of a covenant in which we experience God's love, mercy, and forgiveness. Our faith in that kind of a God helps us to form a conscience. Living according to our conscience is living the covenant. And living the covenant will make us free.

28.
THE COVENANT IN THE LIFE OF BODILY CREATURES

Perhaps we should begin by defining a covenant. A covenant is similar to a contract with one major exception. In a contract, there is not necessarily a relationship between the two people involved. Once you sign a contract to sell your house, you have no need to have a relationship with the buyer ever again. It is over and done with. In a covenant, one takes on a relationship that lasts as long as the covenant lasts. A covenant is a day-to-day working and living relationship with mutual responsibilities and benefits for both parties involved.

In the story of Abraham, the covenant finds blessing with numerous descendants. God tells Abraham that in his descendants all nations of the earth shall find blessing (Genesis 22:18). The key word in this blessing is "all." All nations are not blessed because of their numerical enormity, but in their diversity. In other words, not just Israel, but all nations; not just Jews, but Arabs; not just white, but black as well. Diversity receives God's blessing.

We could even say with limited assurance that diversity is God's will. No one can deny that diversity is a fact—look around you...No two people look or are alike; no two minds think exactly alike; no two lilies are the same; no two snowflakes are the same shape; and on and on... Diversity is God's gift to each one of us—the beauty of being different and not the predictability and boredom of all being the same. Diversity is God's will for us—a challenge to learning and the spice of excitement and surprise. Leo Buscaglia, the famed lecturer on "love," once said that "learning leads to change; change leads to surprise; and surprise leads to joy!" The joy of diversity—the beauty of being different—the excitement of something unique! Even for those who deny the existence of God, diversity still remains a fact. For those of us who do believe in God, we are slowly learning to discover God within life's diversity. The entire New Testament is a literary struggle to deal with the man, Jesus, and how diverse and different he was from other Jews, other prophets and other sons of God.

Diversity, then, is not something we should fear, but welcome with open hearts and minds and arms. Diversity, then, is not something we should diminish, but enhance with acceptance and understanding.

This leads us, then, to recognizing and reflecting upon the diversity we find in human sexuality and sexual lifestyles. Sexual diversity in humanity is not as simple as it used to be. There was a time when man meant male and woman meant female. Today, psychology has helped us see that in a man, there is both male and female, and in a woman, there is both male and female. Today we are learning that even this paradox is not the end of our sexual diversity, but only the beginning. We live in a world where not only men are sexually attracted to women (and vice versa), but also where women are sexually attracted to other women and men are sexually attracted to other men. We are slowly learning that what we once defined as sexually or bodily "natural" has many loopholes. We come from a cultural past that called celibacy, "supernatural"; being single, "unnatural"; and being married, "natural." How differently we see these lifestyles today!

It is the diversity of all people that leads to the need for discipline and laws, and consequently institutions to promote discipline and protect this diversity.

In our tradition, there are two institutions that govern our lives in all matters relating to the covenant. These two institutions cause us to ask two questions, then, in relation to sexuality: The two institutions are Judaism and Christianity. The two questions are:
1. What do the Hebrew Scriptures say about sex?
2. What do the Christian Scriptures say about sex?

The first question: What do the Hebrew Scriptures say about sex? As you all know, the Ten Commandments given through Moses spell out in concrete terms how Israel hoped to fulfill their part of the covenant. Through the Commandments or the Law (the Torah), Israel could discipline its members in order to protect the whole community—for it was the whole community that God brought out of slavery and it is the whole community who responds to that salvation (Exodus 20:1-17). Therefore, the Ten Commandments are communal and not individual—they are set up to protect the good order and proper running of the chosen community. Transgression against the Law was considered a transgression against the covenant community. Transgression against the covenant community is transgression against God. Israel and God become united in the covenant. Any violation of the Law is a scar in the covenant. You may have noticed that there are two Commandments concerning sexual activity: "You shall not commit adultery." "You shall not covet your neighbor's wife." Knowing that the Law is set up to protect the community, we can conclude that these laws on sexuality are also set up to protect the good order of the community and thus their relationship to God. Adultery, then, is not spoken of in the Bible as an objective evil in itself, but only insofar as it destroys trust and relationships among the families within the covenant community. Coveting your neighbor's wife is certainly detrimental to the good order of small tribal communities, as the Jews were built on the family and tribal traditions. The sin, then, is not strictly adultery or fornication or coveting your neighbor's wife, but rather the breaking down of the Covenant Community through such disruptive acts. The sin is not one of disobedience against God, but one of harming the body of the community. If there is no community, there is no covenant! God does not make a covenant with individuals, but with all people. We are all in this together. The Hebrew Scriptures, then, teach us that the sexual act is not a private affair, but one that is social and communal, and reaches out far beyond the two persons engaged in that act.

The second question: What do the Christian Scriptures say about sex? In Israel at the time of Jesus, the temple was the place where God's Law was found. In all four Gospels, Jesus cleanses the temple of its sinners and sin in order to prepare a place for his Body, the Church. In one grand swoop, Jesus prophetically gestures to his Church the need to respect the Law by respecting the place where that Law is found. That place is the temple. And the temple symbolizes all people through whom and with whom God makes a covenant. Notice what John the Evangelist says: "Actually he was talking about the Temple of his Body" (John 2:21).

Jesus calls the temple his Body. The New Testament calls the Church the "Body of Christ" and all Christians "Temples of The Holy Spirit." And so the Law given by God to Israel lives on in us too, the Church of Jesus Christ, which has come to be called "Christianity."

To understand the sometimes extreme stances of Christianity on various sexual issues, we must place ourselves in the capable hands of the Church's moral theologians. Moral theology within Christianity has a long, complicated, and revered history. Over the centuries, many principles, rules, guidelines, and laws have emerged following endless debates on countless moral issues. However, two principles have remained constant throughout these centuries: The first principle is that of **conscience**: If a person clearly believes that he or she is living according to conscience and not committing a sin, then that is morally acceptable within Christian tradition. Seeing something as an evil doesn't mean that everyone who does it is committing a sin. We must learn to separate an evil from a sin. The second principle is that of **dissent**: A person can raise the question about the teaching of Christianity or the principle involved. In both positions (conscience and dissent), Christianity holds up the value while at the same time acts out of compassion. Our moral system in Christianity is a balance of challenge with compassion.

Therefore, Christians alongside the Jews are the covenant communities chosen by God. Jews are the Body of Israel, heirs of Moses and the prophets, the synagogue, saved by God. Christians are the Body of Christ, temples of the Holy Spirit, the Church, saved by God's Son. Christians alongside the Jews are the **people of God!**

29.
GOOD AND EVIL

The destruction of Jerusalem was one of the darkest moments in the history of Israel. The death of Jesus was one of the darkest events in the life of the twelve apostles. Jesus spoke to Nicodemus about the goodness of the light and the evil of darkness (John Chapter 3).

Israel cherished these images of darkness and light to express all the mysteries of good and evil they experienced. The first Christians, who were Jews, continued the use of these images and we hold them in our tradition to the present day. Sin is always darkness! Virtue is always light!

What is the bridge that fills the gap from darkness to light? What did it take for Israel to overcome the destruction of Jerusalem and exile? What transpired between the crucifixion and the resurrection that formed a church?

Jesus answers these questions when he tells Nicodemus that whoever **believes** possesses the truth. **Faith** determines the forces of history! **Faith** orders the life of cultures, peoples, and individuals! **Faith** is that journey from darkness to light; from exile to freedom; from crucifixion to resurrection; from death to life; from sin to virtue!

Too long has our world hidden speaking about sex and sexuality in dark places, behind closed doors, in low whispered sounds. What do you think we conveyed from generation to generation about sex? You guessed it—based on our images—we saw sex as evil, as sin, the unmentionable subject; only to be used in procreation. Our negative views of sex and sexuality come from ourselves (certainly not from God).

Every once in a while in the history of humanity a spring cleaning is experienced; a breath of fresh air gushes through the stagnation; freedom comes to the oppressed; light shines in the darkness; a revolution produces good! I believe that has happened in our own time. We call it the Sexual Revolution! Over the past forty years, the world has begun again to groan for redemption. How could such a beautiful expression of love and marriage, which feels so good, produces so much good, be wrong or sinful?! The Revolution says that sex is good, that the body is good. But then, so does the Bible; so does the Church. This Revolution is not our own doing, but the work of God—the same God who, after creating our sexuality, blessed it with the words: Indeed, it is good (Genesis 1:27-31)! However, what is it going to take to keep it in the light and from retreating back into the closet or dark corners of the future? The answer, of course, is **faith!**

But only people can have faith. That means it is up to us. It is especially up to us who claim to be believers...People who take the risks that faith demands: discussing and dialoguing openly about our sexuality; teaching our children about the goodness and beauty of our bodies; showing each other affection and love in sexual gestures (touching, kissing, embracing, holding someone's hand).

If we believe in our sexuality, and that it is good, then it is up to **us** to keep that dream alive!

30.
THE MYSTERY OF LOVE

Reading: I Corinthians 13:1-13

Just because you're patient and kind doesn't mean you're in love... Just because you're always ready to excuse and never selfish doesn't mean you're in love...These are personality traits...A criminal can love...A rude, impatient person is capable of loving...The extrovert loves as well as the introvert...Love is **not** a personality trait!

Just because I can prophesy or speak eloquently doesn't mean I can be in love...Just because I know all there is to know and am the greatest of philosophers doesn't mean I can be in love...These are the results of the intellect...A dumb person can be in love...An uneducated person is capable of loving...The ignorant love as well as scholars...Love is **not** knowledge!

Just because I don't get jealous and am not resentful doesn't mean I can love...Just because I don't get angry and never get depressed doesn't mean I can love...These are emotions...One can mourn out of love...One can laugh out of love...Sinners love as well as saints...Love is **not** an emotion!

Just because I am in good physical condition and physically attractive doesn't mean I am a lover...Just because I can have and desire sex doesn't mean I am a lover...Sex is physical...Good health is physical...An ugly person can love as well as a beautiful person...The impotent can love as well as the potent...Love is **not** physical!

We can define a covenant. We can define a wife or a husband. We can define patience. We can define endurance, as does St. Paul. We can define marriage. But we cannot define love!

If love is neither a personality trait, nor an emotion, nor knowledge, nor physical, nor definable—what is it?

Love is a mystery!...And like all mysteries cannot be proven nor defined! Like the mystery of life, we can love with or without knowledge, sick or healthy, rich or poor, emotional or unemotional, beautiful or ugly, brilliant or obtuse, thin or fat, generous or selfish, meek or aggressive. Like life, love is possible despite the infinite diversity of the lover. Like life, love thrives on diversity and is not diminished nor extinguished by it.

But just because love is a mystery, which is indefinable, doesn't mean we cannot say something about love—of course we can, just as we do about life. St. Paul did. Let's see what he said:

St. Paul in his letter to the Corinthians, says: "There is no limit to love's forbearance...its power to endure." But he adds: "There are in the end, three things that last: faith, hope, and love, and the greatest of these is love." For Paul, the essential ingredients to love are endurance or perseverance, as well as faith and hope.

Because love is a mystery—it is very difficult for two people to be sure whether they are in love or not—fascinated with each other, yes—infatuated with each other, yes—but in love—who could dare make such a claim?

To be in love is not discernable with the intellect or the emotions—it takes one's total being—and that takes faith. I can only believe I am in love—I can never be sure. I can hope I'm in love—I can never know. What love is can be known only by loving! And who can ever be sure he or she is loving? Notice how today's generation says "Let's make love" when they want to have sex together. What a misnomer! "Let's have sex" would be more accurate. Or we hear people say, "Prove that you love me by marrying me." With the high divorce rate in today's society, marriage is no proof of anything!

Sex is not love—marriage is not love—these are definable in themselves. They are different from love, yet they are the expressions of love, not to be confused with love itself! Sex is not love, like walking is not life. One need not be able to walk in order to live. One need not have sex in order to love. Therefore, referring to sex as love diminishes the mystery to a single act. The mystery of love is tangibly expressed through our sexuality, but is not the same as sex.

If LOVE is a mystery, with only FAITH and HOPE as its basis (indefinable, unfathomable, unprovable)—is there ever a moment in the life of two people when they could say with any surety that they are in love?...Yes—at the moment of death! Did you ever notice that there is only one condition spoken in the marriage vows of all traditions—"until death"? Love can be built only on PERSEVERANCE. And the only kind of person who can do this is one who has FAITH.

Perseverance is the nearest guarantee we have to the mystery of love. If it is love, then it is eternal. "There is no limit to love's power to endure." We, who are human, and must die, will experience love most at that moment—the moment of death—the moment of perseverance.

Sex is something you do. Sexuality is something we have. Both are the bodily medium through which the mystery of love is expressed and experienced. We are human. We are, therefore, bodies and spirits. We have the full capacity to **LOVE!**

714206